T0215330

"*Digital Transformation in Your Manufacturing Business: A Made Smarter Guide* distils over 5 years of Made Smarter experience working with thousands of manufacturing companies across every sector. The accessible yet comprehensive descriptions of the technologies will help leaders at any stage of their digital transformation journey".

Donna Edwards, *Managing Director,*
The Growth Company

"A practical insight exploring how to combine the fundamentals of people and technology, and deliver a manufacturing sector fit for the modern world. *Digital Transformation in Your Manufacturing Business: A Made Smarter Guide* is a must-read for anyone who wants to get ahead of the curve, leading and shaping change, rather than being carried along by it".

Philippa Glover, *UK industrialist*

"An excellent starting point for anyone interested in manufacturing technology wanting to know how industry 4.0 can accelerate the growth of their business. *Digital Transformation in Your Manufacturing Business: A Made Smarter Guide* is a must-have book for any manufacturing leader".

Alain Dilworth, *Made Smarter Programme Manager*

Digital Transformation in Your Manufacturing Business

Are you a manufacturing leader and unsure of which technology can help grow your business? Have you heard about 3D printing, Industry 4.0, robots, or artificial intelligence but don't know how they can be used in manufacturing?

This book gives a clear and practical guide to manufacturing technologies, providing examples of how they're used, as well as the tools and techniques you'll need to get started. Each technology is covered in a brief and simple way allowing you to understand it quickly and decide if it's worth investigating for your business.

In addition to this book, the online resources will provide you with templates and examples to help you get started. At every stage there are suggestions for the key terms you will need to find more information appropriate to your industry.

This isn't just about technology, it's a roadmap for your digital transformation. Start with guidance on setting your company's vision and direction, to getting the people in your business engaged and ready to adopt technology. Move on to exploring each of the technologies, and the tools and techniques you'll find useful along the way. Finally, connect the technologies with the tools that are appropriate, and look at common issues in manufacturing businesses and how these can be resolved.

Get started with making informed decisions, embracing technologies, and transforming your business.

Will Kinghorn is the automation and robotics specialist for the Made Smarter Adoption Programme, where he advises and supports manufacturing companies with the introduction of new technologies.

After graduating from Loughborough University with a master's degree in Product Design and Manufacture, he worked in the aerospace industry for more than a decade. There, he developed and implemented new manufacturing techniques including automation, robotics, advanced machining, inspection, and welding in a range of production facilities. He is a chartered manufacturing engineer with the Institution of Mechanical Engineers (IMechE).

Digital Transformation in Your Manufacturing Business

A Made Smarter Guide

Will Kinghorn

CRC Press
Taylor & Francis Group
Boca Raton London New York

CRC Press is an imprint of the
Taylor & Francis Group, an **informa** business

Cover image: Image 1462012340 used under license from Shutterstock.com. Use of the Made Smarter logo has been granted by the Made Smarter programme.

First edition published 2024
by CRC Press
2385 NW Executive Center Drive, Suite 320, Boca Raton FL 33431

and by CRC Press
4 Park Square, Milton Park, Abingdon, Oxon, OX14 4RN

CRC Press is an imprint of Taylor & Francis Group, LLC

© 2024 Will Kinghorn

Library of Congress Cataloging-in-Publication Data
Name: Kinghorn, Will, author.
Title: Digital transformation in your manufacturing business :
a made smarter guide / Will Kinghorn.
Description: 1 edition. | Boca Raton, FL : Taylor & Francis, 2024. |
Includes bibliographical references and index.
Identifiers: LCCN 2023053780 (print) | LCCN 2023053781 (ebook) |
ISBN 9781032642208 (hardback) | ISBN 9781032626246 (paperback) |
ISBN 9781032642215 (ebook)
Subjects: LCSH: Manufacturing industries. |
Manufactures–Technological innovations. |
Manufacturing processes–Technological innovations.
Classification: LCC HD9720.5 .K576 2024 (print) |
LCC HD9720.5 (ebook) | DDC 338/.064–dc23/eng/20240126
LC record available at https://lccn.loc.gov/2023053780
LC ebook record available at https://lccn.loc.gov/2023053781

ISBN: 9781032642208 (hbk)
ISBN: 9781032626246 (pbk)
ISBN: 9781032642215 (ebk)

DOI: 10.1201/9781032642215

Typeset in Minion
by Newgen Publishing UK

Access the Support Material: www.routledge.com/9781032626246

Contents

Foreword

IHAVE BEEN WORKING IN THE MANUFACTURING SECTOR FOR OVER 35 YEARS, and when I was the CEO of Siemens UK I was honoured to lead the investigation into the state of technology utilisation in British industry, which led to the Made Smarter Review in 2017. This was the start of the Made Smarter brand and a range of business support which began with the Made Smarter Adoption pilot programme in the North West of England in 2019.

I am delighted that since then, the growth and impact of the movement has been exciting, reaching thousands of companies of all sizes through Made Smarter Innovation, skills programmes, research centres, hubs, and the expansion of the Adoption programme into five additional regions.

However, there is still work to be done. Many companies haven't experienced the improvement in productivity, profitability, and efficiency which digitalisation provides. This can be due to several reasons, but often it's because business leaders are time-poor and need to focus on the day-to-day aspects of the business. Combine this with the perception that they need to be experts in robotics or virtual reality in order to make it successful, and it's easy to see why such projects get pushed further down the to-do list.

This is where Made Smarter Adoption helps, by providing access to skilled, independent advisors who can guide, support, and inform manu-facturing leaders, the companies can embrace new technologies, upskill staff, and accelerate growth.

Will Kinghorn is a leading technology advisor specialising in robotics and automation for the North West region. Prior to that he worked in the aerospace sector developing and implementing pioneering manufacturing technologies. He has worked with more than 100 SME manufacturers, identifying issues, recommending solutions, and supporting the business leaders with the development and implementation of projects. His first-hand experience provides the foundation for this book – the fact that many issues are common across industries and sectors, and while the solutions will vary, the approach to solving them is similar. This book provides an introduction to this approach, allowing business leaders to make an informed decision about what is right for their business and helping them be an intelligent customer when dealing with technology suppliers and support agencies.

Throughout my career I have witnessed first-hand the benefits that digitalisation brings to a company regardless of size and sector. But with SME manufacturers being such a crucial part of the economy, now is the time to encourage and support them in their technology adoption journey.

We're in the midst of the fourth industrial revolution, Industry 4.0, which is driven by digitalisation. The innovators and early adopters are reaping the benefits, now we need to spread the word to the hundreds of thousands of SME manufacturers and seize upon the revolutionary movement.

For you, or someone you know, working as a leader in a manufacturing company, this book is the perfect start of the journey.

Prof. Juergen Maier CBE, FRS,
Founder of Made Smarter
November 2023

Acknowledgements

Thank you in particular to Donna, Kevin, and Alain from the MADE Smarter Adoption programme for being so supportive of this project from the start and for providing constructive suggestions at each stage. I'm grateful to Cheryl and Lucy for their time reviewing and advising me on important parts of this book. I've also learned a great deal from the rest of the team: Claire, Danielle, Ian, Jan, Jess, Joan, Jonathan, Jude, Michael, Ruth, Sarah, and Steve. Plenty of their knowledge and experience has made its way into this book. Finally, thank you to Liz for all the encouragement, and to Izzy and Zoe for providing motivation by asking when my story about the robot will be finished.

Introduction

WHAT IS DIGITALISATION?

In many aspects of our lives we have seen technologies emerge and develop which change how we do things, in both our work and our private lives. In recent decades the majority of digital technologies have been driven by improvements in computing power, allowing more complicated things to be done faster and more efficiently.

The move from analogue to digital is the process of digitalisation, which has come to mean using a computer or computer processing to complete tasks which were previously done by hand, or not done at all. An everyday example is the camera. Film cameras were replaced by the development of digital cameras, and thanks to the advances in computing and battery power, most people now use their mobile phone as their main camera. This is digitalisation, but it also extends to how we manage, edit, store, and share our photos – slide projectors and holiday photo prints have largely been replaced with online albums, sharing on social media, and viewing and editing photos on a phone or tablet.

As a leader of a manufacturing business it can be difficult to keep track of the development of technologies which are appropriate to your industry, and with the everyday pressures of running a business the temptation is to keep on doing things the same way. As with photography, the improvements in computing power have the potential to revolutionise your manufacturing business, and indeed it already has in many companies.

The purpose of this book is to introduce these technologies and quickly explain how they can improve productivity, quality, and profitability, or

DOI: 10.1201/9781032642215-1

1

whatever your current issues are, and allow you to make an informed decision about which are right for your business.

HOW TO USE THIS BOOK

Every manufacturing company is different, with different issues and challenges, ambitions and goals, and there isn't a one-size-fits-all approach to digitalisation. You don't have to spend hours reading this from cover to cover; look up the technology you've heard about and you'll find a section for each technology with a brief introduction to it, an explanation of the benefits and drawbacks, as well as some typical uses. This will give you an idea if it's a good fit for your company, and at the end of each topic there are some suggestions for search terms you can use online to investigate it further.

Any given technology is unlikely to solve your problems on its own; you will need your staff to be engaged and supportive of the change. To help with this, Chapter 1 explains how to establish your company's purpose which is key to working out which technology to implement first and more importantly allowing you to engage with your staff and get their support. Chapter 2 provides guidance on how to get the most out of your staff throughout the whole process. Chapter 3 covers the technologies, and Chapter 4 provides tools and techniques which will help you along the way, again, you won't need all of these so pick the ones most relevant to you. Chapter 5 shows which tools and techniques are appropriate for each technology, as well as linking common issues in manufacturing businesses with steps to resolve them.

WHAT IS MADE SMARTER IN THE UK?

Made Smarter was created following an industry-led review of how UK manufacturing industries can prosper through digital tools and innovation. This independent review[1] was commissioned by UK government and led by Professor Juergen Maier CBE, Co-Chair of Made Smarter. The review made four key recommendations covering leadership, adoption, innovation, and skills.

The movement has grown into an array of nationwide support opportunities for businesses including funding for research and development, support with collaboration, commercialising technologies through research centres, establishing innovation hubs, and developing standards.

The Made Smarter Adoption programme provides support to small- and medium-sized enterprise (SME) manufacturers in the form of impartial business growth advice, specialist technology advice, guidance for skills and culture development, funding opportunities, and leadership development.

NOTE

1 Maier, J. *Made smarter review*. UK Industrial Digitalisation Review, 2017.

BIBLIOGRAPHY

Maier, J. *Made smarter review*. UK Industrial Digitalisation Review, 2017.

CHAPTER 1

Establishing Your Company's Purpose

DIGITAL TRANSFORMATION

What Is It?

It is the process of digitalising elements of a business to enable improvements, usually in efficiency, profitability, productivity, or expanding the services offered to customers. It can be applied to any area of the business, such as moving from a paper order book to an online service so that the information can be accessed by whoever needs it, wherever they are, through to upgrading machines to gather information on how well they run or how much power they use.

In general, embracing technology which supports staff with their tasks will allow them to focus on the more interesting and profitable parts of their job, because the mundane tasks are taken care of automatically, or they've been given easy access to information they didn't have before which makes them more effective.

How Do I Do It?

It can be easy to get drawn into particular technologies and then try to find a use for them, but this will often end up with systems not being used and

DOI: 10.1201/9781032642215-2

ultimately losing money. A more reliable approach is to look for the issues facing your business and then research appropriate technologies which will help you solve those problems. This is technology pull rather than technology push.

- Establish your company's direction. This is an important first step as this will help frame what you need to do.
- Identify the issues that are preventing your business from meeting its targets, such as new equipment required to enter new markets, lack of capacity in the sales team preventing them winning more customers, or recruitment issues preventing an increase in production capacity.
- Prioritise these issues and select the one which will provide the biggest benefit.
- Discuss the issues with staff and stakeholders to provide more information and improve engagement.
- Research options to solve the issues. These may not be specific technologies, but tools and techniques as well.
- Create a plan and allocate people the time and resources needed to be successful.
- Take the issues one by one, and regularly review and share progress.

What Are the Benefits and Limitations?

- ✓ Improved efficiency, profitability, and productivity.
- ✓ Opens new opportunities in markets and products.
- ✓ Improved staff engagement and job satisfaction.
- – It can be difficult to prioritise, use business cases ('Building a Business Case' section) and a technology roadmap ('Technology Strategy/ Roadmap' section).
- – Knowledge may not exist in the company, see 'Where to go for Technical Support'.

Useful Search Terms

- Digital transformation examples in <<industry>>.
- SME digital transformation.
- Industry 4.0 in <<industry>> or <<manufacturing process>>.

COMPANY STRATEGY/BUSINESS PLAN/BUSINESS MODEL

What Is It?

It is a document explaining the purpose and direction of your company over the coming years, depending on the type of business this could be as little as the next one to two years, or up to 10 or 25 years in the future. The business model can be a brief document, and it doesn't have to be endless pages of tables and market research. The idea is to quickly explain to stakeholders what your business does and where you want it to go in the future. The strategy is the approach you and the company will take to achieve this, and the business plan is a more detailed document normally produced to share with potential investors. The priorities should be the business model and the strategy.

Key elements should be shared with staff and stakeholders so that they understand the company that they're involved in and can see how any proposed changes fit in the bigger picture. Employees are likely to be more committed to a company that shares their beliefs and values. Some key areas to include are:

- A summary of what the company makes, where it is based, and any key people and their roles.
- Description of the markets the business operates in, key customers, processes, and key suppliers.
- Current metrics such as turnover or sales volumes, and ambitions for the growth of these along with specific targets and the expected year they will be achieved.
- The values and ethics of the business.
- Approaches which will be used, such as agile, continuous improvement, or lean manufacturing.
- Important pledges or accreditation, for example, net zero targets, ISO14001, or United Kingdom Accreditation Service (UKAS) traceability.
- Commitment to review and update the strategy on specific dates or following significant changes such as acquiring new businesses, global events, or leadership changes.

How Do I Do It?

Depending on the structure of your business you may want to include key stakeholders such as the leadership team, owners, investors, or staff representatives in the creation of the strategy.

- Start by briefly describing the current state of the business and its products and services.
- Involve the leadership team and employees to identify important values and ethics.
- Review the financial position and agree a baseline for metrics such as turnover or profit before tax.
- Describe any strengths, weaknesses, opportunities, and threats (SWOT).
- Decide on development or improvement areas, such as new products, new markets, or a new service offering like aftercare or a feature unique to your company.
- Create and agree realistic and numeric targets.
- Outline the steps needed to achieve these targets, including dates.
- Commit to a date to review and reissue the document. There are many strategies and frameworks available; some are suitable for particular situations, so use any which suit your business, and change the approach if it makes sense after the review.
- Summarise the key points in language appropriate for the audience, and brief staff and stakeholders.

What Are the Benefits and Limitations?

- ✓ Clarity of the business's purpose and values.
- ✓ Improved decision-making.
- ✓ Improved employee engagement.
- – It can be difficult knowing where to start, particularly when a business has grown organically. Start with a few brief descriptions and ambitions, discuss these with people in the business and add more detail as needed.

Useful Search Terms
- SME business model guide/template/prompts.
- SWOT analysis template.

TECHNOLOGY STRATEGY/TECHNOLOGY ROADMAP

What Is It?

It is a description of the technology projects the business needs to undertake, and when, in order to achieve the business's objectives. Similar to the business model, it doesn't need to be a lengthy document, rather a clear list of technologies which will be acquired, developed, or investigated over the same time period as the business model. This can be easily shared with stakeholders and staff to explain why a project is important and how it will benefit the business, helping to improve staff engagement and retention.

In order to improve the clarity of the technology strategy, the rationale for each technology should include:

- When the project needs to be completed, ideally along with how long it will take.
- Which business metric(s) and current issues the project will improve. For example, in order to improve productivity in the sales team, new order management software is required.
- Which elements of the business model it will enable. For example, "a new piece of machinery is required to access a particular market and grow the business". Or, "in order to develop our next new product, we need to develop a method of updating products remotely".

How Do I Do It?

Involve key stakeholders in the creation of the strategy as this will help to provide a more robust and effective plan.

- Review the business model and list any obvious technology requirements.
- Add any improvement ideas and projects raised from staff engagement sessions or longer-term actions raised from day-to-day operations.
- Use the business metrics or key performance indicators as a scoring system and categorise the impact each technology or project is likely to have on these metrics.

- Prioritise them according to impact.
- Display them on a timeline showing when they are required to complete.
- Allocate resource to the highest priority projects, allowing the person the time in their day job to complete the tasks.
- Regularly review progress with the active projects (see the 'Project Management' or 'Agile Project Management' sections) and agree a review period for the strategy.

What Are the Benefits and Limitations?

- ✓ Projects are more likely to successfully help the business achieve its goals.
- ✓ Improve staff engagement with projects which may otherwise be intimidating.
- ✓ Provides clarity for the business, allowing staff to focus on priority projects rather than undertaking too much.
- – Lack of familiarity with new technologies could make initial judgements difficult. Research the options and if necessary, look for external support, see 'Where to go for Technical Support'.

Useful Search Terms

- Manufacturing technology roadmap examples in <<*industry*>>.
- Technology strategy for SMEs.

KEY PERFORMANCE INDICATORS (KPIS) AND METRICS

What Is It?

It is a series of figures which quickly give an indication of how areas of the business, or the business as a whole, are performing. The chosen metrics need to be relevant and have a direct relationship with the performance of the business in terms of the business model. The metrics or indicators can be different in each area of the business, and the most important from each area becomes a key process indicator (KPI), which is monitored at a higher level in the business. For example:

- The sales team could measure and display weekly totals for number of enquiries, number converted to orders, the conversion rate, the average response time, and the total value of orders year to date. The conversion rate and total order values could be selected as KPIs.

- The manufacturing team could measure the scrap rate, number of products delivered, percentage of products delivered on time, overall equipment effectiveness (OEE), energy use, and the cycle time of important operations. The OEE and number of products delivered could be selected as KPIs.

- At the monthly board meeting the leadership team would then discuss performance based around the sales conversion rate, total order value, OEE, and products delivered.

Ideally all the KPIs would be automatically updated from the software systems used to run the business and displayed on dashboards in the relevant area, but in most cases this isn't possible yet, so displaying them on a whiteboard is a workable solution. If the data isn't quickly available and requires someone to manually collate and analyse it before displaying it, then establishing a way to simplify this process should be a priority.

How Do I Do It?

Select metrics which will best align with the company's growth targets and business model. The rate at which they are updated, how they are measured, where they are displayed, and how often they are reviewed all need to be agreed in advance to avoid ambiguity.

Each business is different so there isn't an ideal number of metrics for each area, but too many can be overwhelming and confusing to people not regularly involved in the details, while too few can miss important information. A common way of structuring metrics is to use the following themes, or variations on safety, quality, cost, delivery, and people (SQCDP); these could be reviewed daily with the shop floor team for the first 15 minutes of a shift so everybody is clear on current performance.

What Are the Benefits and Limitations?

- ✓ Quickly track progress.
- ✓ Improved stakeholder confidence.
- ✓ Enables effective business cases.
- − Context is important when displaying figures; make sure people understand why they are there and what they mean.

 – It can lead to micromanaging; be mindful of this when reviewing the metrics and look at the behaviours in the business that the metrics drive.

Useful Search Terms

- Manufacturing KPIs in <<*industry*>>.
- SQCDP board example.

BUILDING A BUSINESS CASE

What Is It?

It is a way of showing the overall benefits of a project or technology, allowing you to make an informed decision on whether to go ahead with it or not. When looking at a number of projects in different areas, using a business case will help you to objectively compare them and then decide where to focus limited funding and resources. The criteria used should be more than just the project cost and the expected payback. For example, adding a safety system to a machine would improve the health and safety of the workforce but wouldn't necessarily have a direct impact on the business's income, making the return on investment look poor for a project which is obviously beneficial.

For a small manufacturer the business case doesn't need to be pages of complex calculations; it just needs to show the criteria that are important to the business, and then include a method of scoring or evaluating each project against these criteria. A single page of A4 should be enough to capture a summary of:

- What the project is.
- The project's aims.
- The main benefits.
- The risks to the project.
- A measure of how likely the project is to be successful.
- Who will run the project, who else needs to be involved, and how long it will take.
- Likely costs.
- A score for the project against the pre-agreed criteria.

How Do I Do It?

The selected criteria need to align to the business model so that the projects which will have the most impact on the company meeting its targets score the highest and are more likely to be enacted. This is related to company strategy and key performance indicators, covered earlier in this chapter.

- Identify and agree the metrics to be used for assessing every project.
- Create a standard template or a list of prompts, with a scoring matrix so all projects are judged against the same standard.
- Allow people the time to create the business cases for potential projects.
- Explore the potential impacts on each metric for the projects.
- Estimate the value of these and summarise them or score them using the scoring matrix.
- Review each business case as a leadership team and agree which projects to progress with.

What Are the Benefits and Limitations?

- ✓ Select the projects which will have the biggest benefit for the company.
- ✓ Objectively compare projects in different areas or with different benefits.
- ✓ Focus limited funds effectively.
- − It can be difficult to score some projects against set criteria, so context is important, in this case discuss with the leadership team and check that the criteria are appropriate or if they need refining.
- − It can feel pointless for projects which on the first look are obvious requirements, but the process can shed light on potential difficulties, shortfalls, or opportunities which need addressing.

Useful Search Terms

- Business case criteria examples.
- Net present value (NPV).
- Return on investment (ROI).
- Project risk assessment.

NET ZERO

What Is It?

It is the state when the amount of greenhouse gas emissions going into the atmosphere are balanced by the same amount of greenhouse gases being removed from the atmosphere. A net zero plan should be a key part of a business model.

It is critical for every business to understand their emissions, create a plan, and then execute it in order to reduce their emissions to net zero. This will restrict the average increase in the Earth's temperature resulting from climate change. In doing so, your company will also find that machines are more efficient, energy costs are lower, supply chains are more resilient, compliance with legislation is easier, and staff retention is improved.

A business's emissions are normally split into:[1]

- The direct emissions from things like gas boilers or company vehicles, called scope 1 emissions.
- The indirect emissions released through the generation of any electricity your business uses, called scope 2 emissions.
- All other emissions generated throughout the value chain, including things such as the mining of the raw materials used in your products, the emissions from your employees commuting to work, and the disposal of your products at the end of their life. These are called scope 3 emissions.

Different gases contribute to the greenhouse effect by different amounts, for example, methane is 28 times[2] more potent than carbon dioxide, and so carbon dioxide equivalent (CO_2e) is used as a standard unit to help with calculations. When calculating your annual emissions you'll convert everything to CO_2e and report it in tonnes. For example, if your air conditioning system leaked 1 kg of refrigerant gas in a year, this would add 3.9 tonnes CO_2e onto your scope 1 emissions.

How Do I Do It?

Making your company net zero is a long-term goal, and will require regular actions and planning. Start by adding net zero to the agenda for every board meeting or monthly leadership meeting, so that it gets regular attention. Discuss your intentions with your staff to see if any of them have an interest in the topic and would like to help with the projects.

The first step is to measure your emissions, with scopes 1 and 2 being relatively easy – look at your electricity and gas bills, any fuel receipts from company vehicles, and maintenance logs to check for air conditioning fluid top-ups in the last year. Online tools are available to help you convert these figures into annual tonnes of CO_2e. Scope 3 will be more involved and the online tools will guide you through some questions to get an initial estimate, but look into the categories that make up scope 3 and then identify the areas which are likely to be largest for you, and focus on those initially.

Once you have an idea of your annual emissions, make a public pledge stating the target date for when you will reach net zero. For example, the UK government has committed to reach net zero by 2050,[3] and the Greater Manchester authority has committed to 2038[4] – it will take time, but the important thing is to start with some actions rather than spending time calculating every source of CO_2e.

Create an overview plan for the business reaching net zero. Even if you don't have all the answers yet, this will take research and development. Consider putting money aside each year for carbon offsetting as an interim measure, just make sure any carbon offsetting schemes are accredited and will only sell each offset unit once. To achieve net zero, offsetting should account for less than 10% of total emissions.

What Are the Benefits and Limitations?

- ✓ Reduced energy costs, more resilient supply chains, and reduced waste.
- ✓ Improve the public image of the company, attract new and engage staff, while contributing to addressing climate change.
- ✓ Regulations are already in place for large companies, and due to the nature of scope 3 these will pass down the supply chain, starting now will make compliance to regulations simpler.
- – A complex topic and some sources of carbon emissions are currently unavoidable, any net zero plan will likely take years, so focus on what is available and achievable now while planning for the future.

Useful Search Terms

- Business carbon emissions calculator.
- Net zero/carbon reduction schemes in <<location>> or <<industry>>.

- SME net zero support in <<*location*>>.
- Net zero regulations in <<*location*>> or <<*industry*>>.

NOTES

1 World Business Council for Sustainable Development. *The Greenhouse Gas Protocol: A corporate accounting and reporting standard.* World Business Council for Sustainable Development, 2004.

2 Department for Energy Security and Net Zero 2023. *Greenhouse gas reporting: Conversion factors 2023.* Available at www.gov.uk/government/publi cations/greenhouse-gas-reporting-conversion-factors-2023

3 UK Government Climate Change Act 2008. Available at www.legislation.gov. uk/ukpga/2008/27/contents

4 Greater Manchester Combined Authority. *5-year environment plan for Greater Manchester.* Greater Manchester Combined Authority, 2019. Available at www. greatermanchester-ca.gov.uk/what-we-do/environment/five-year-environm ent-plan/

BIBLIOGRAPHY

Carbon Trust. *The journey to net zero for SMEs guide.* Carbon Trust, 2022.

Department for Energy Security and Net Zero 2023. *Greenhouse gas reporting: Conversion factors 2023.* Available at www.gov.uk/government/ publications/greenhouse-gas-reporting-conversion-factors-2023/

Greater Manchester Combined Authority. *5-year environment plan for Greater Manchester.* Greater Manchester Combined Authority, 2019. Available at www.greatermanchester-ca.gov.uk/what-we-do/environment/five-year-environment-plan/

Osterwalder, A and Pigneur, Y. *Business model generation: A handbook for visionaries, game changers, and challengers.* John Wiley & Sons, 2010.

Pineda, AC, Chang, A and Faria, P. *Foundations for science-based net-zero target setting in the corporate sector.* Science Based Targets Initiative, 2020.

World Business Council for Sustainable Development. *The Greenhouse Gas Protocol: A corporate accounting and reporting standard.* World Business Council for Sustainable Development, 2004.

UK Business Climate Hub. *7 steps to Sustainability.* July 2023. https://business climatehub.uk/7-steps-to-sustainability/

UK Government Climate Change Act 2008. Available at www.legislation.gov.uk/ukpga/2008/27/contents

CHAPTER 2

People and Workforce

ROLES AND RESPONSIBILITIES

What Is It?

It is a written definition of each role in the business, outlining what the person doing that role is expected to do, and what they are accountable for. This provides clarity for employees and the leadership team because everyone understands who is meant to be doing what task, and who to talk to with any issues or concerns. A role is a job title and where it sits within the organisation structure, drawing and displaying this makes it clear how the business is setup and what the reporting lines are. The responsibilities are the tasks and success measures that someone in a particular role is expected to complete.

For example, sales director, machine shop team leader, and production manager are all roles and there can be more than one person with these titles, especially when there are multiple shifts in operation. The responsibilities of the production manager would include setting the production plan to meet demand, ensuring the production team have the resources required to do the job, maintaining quality standards, and ensuring compliance with health and safety regulations. Where there is more than one

DOI: 10.1201/9781032642215-3

production manager, they would all have similar responsibilities, with some minor changes where required, for example, the night shift production manager might cover more areas, or the production manager in the inspection department might have slightly different responsibilities to the assembly production manager. These details should be freely available for people in the company to access, so any personal development needs or individual targets shouldn't be included; they should be in a person's performance review which is kept private.

How Do I Do It?

Start by drawing out the organisation chart for the company as it stands, including any vacant roles. Check that this is capable of delivering the business's strategy and achieving the plans and targets. For example, if you plan to enter a new market as part of the strategy to grow the business, who would be responsible for this in their current role, and would they have the time and resources to do it successfully, or is it worth creating a new role which would allow a person to focus on this. Discuss this with the leadership team, and find out what works well in the current structure and what doesn't. For example, if the production area has grown significantly it could be worth dividing it into sections with additional managers or adding team leaders to allow the production manager to delegate certain responsibilities.

For the responsibilities, start with the leadership team and define what they are responsible for, specifically which elements of the company's strategy will they deliver. Discuss this with them and agree the details. In turn they should do the same thing to agree the responsibilities of their team in such a way that it will allow them to successfully deliver their part in the company's strategy.

What Are the Benefits and Limitations?

- ✓ Improved efficiency, job satisfaction, and motivation.
- ✓ Enables delegation which will allow leaders to focus on their jobs, and also encourage progression within the company by stretching and developing staff in a controlled manner.
- ✓ Ensure compliance with many accrediting bodies, either industry-specific or international.

– In some cases what a person does is different to their role definition, or creating a role definition for someone who is involved in everything can be difficult, so keep in mind the business strategy, its objectives, and where they sit in the organisation chart to help structure the role. Other tasks could always be included in their personal development plan.

Useful Search Terms

- Example role definition/responsibilities for <<*job title*>>.
- Workforce development support in <<*location*>>.

SUCCESSION PLANNING

What Is It?

It means identifying the skills which are critical to the successful operation of a business and putting robust plans in place to ensure the business is resilient. Succession planning helps with situations such as a key member of staff approaching retirement and they are the only person in the company who knows how to run a particular machine, or if they are the only person that does the detailed designs for new products. Once that person leaves there will be a skills gap which prevents the company from operating as successfully as it was before, so the aim is to capture the person's knowledge before they leave and transfer it to other members of staff. Succession planning is also beneficial when a business is over-reliant on certain people, which doesn't allow them the time to focus on growing the business or to take holidays and time off, because without them the business struggles.

How Do I Do It?

Look at the roles and tasks which are fundamental to how your business operates and who they're performed by. To help with this think about what sets your company apart from the competition and who is responsible for this during the product development, production, or the delivery of the service you provide. Another useful way is to think about who can cover tasks when certain staff take time off, if there isn't anyone then it's worth thinking about succession planning. Defining or reviewing roles and responsibilities will also help to identify the areas to focus on.

Review current staff for people with similar skills, even if they can't operate to the required level yet or if there are any members of staff with an interest in the subject, or who are in need of growth and career development. These will be good candidates to pass the knowledge on to. Consider adult apprenticeships which can be used to train existing staff, of any age, in new areas and skills.

There is also the option to use interns, apprentices, or graduates from colleges or universities to bring in new skills as well as an awareness or familiarity with technology. This is a good option when you need to create a new role for the task, or if there isn't a suitable candidate currently employed by the company.

The important part of the process is capturing the knowledge from the current specialist. Depending on the tasks they're performing, something as straightforward as writing a standard operating procedure (SOP) or recording videos of them performing a task may be sufficient. For more complex or nuanced processes where experience plays a large part, arranging staff to shadow the person while they're doing the job is more effective. Over time they'll be able to pick up more and more of the tasks themselves. It will be easier to focus on individual tasks at first rather than a full role that someone performs, so think about the important elements of the job and start with those.

Mentoring is a good method of providing guidance and advice to people within the company, especially when they are learning new skills which will be critical to its future success.

What Are the Benefits and Limitations?

- ✓ Improves business resilience by ensuring key tasks can be performed by more than one person.
- ✓ Improves job satisfaction and enables career development and progression for employees.
- – Learning new skills, especially ones which provide your company with the competitive edge, will take time to learn, so plan this in advance and make sure to allow enough time during the working day to do it properly.

Useful Search Terms

- Knowledge capture techniques for <<task>>.
- Adult apprentices/internships/university career departments in <<location>> or <<technology area>>.

CHANGE MANAGEMENT

What Is It?

It is the process of guiding people through a change within the business and helping them to accept and embrace it in a positive way. A change could be something that appears to be minor, but may have a big effect on some people, such as moving the desks or workstations around in an office or a shop floor. Or it could be a larger scale change such as a management restructure or introducing a robot to the production process. In all these cases, understanding the phases of change that people go through, and adapting your approach to implementing change, will make it more likely to succeed.

For example, a company that has been producing steel frames for 30 years and has always used skilled welders to manually assemble and weld the products is considering buying a welding robot. If the welders aren't consulted and a robot welding cell arrives on the shop floor one day, they will probably be concerned about their jobs for the future and will be unlikely to accept and use the new equipment. Applying a change management strategy could include having a discussion at the start of the project, between the leadership team and the welders, to go through how the business is growing and how automating part of the welding process will help to sustain this growth. It allows the welders to raise any concerns and make suggestions. Keeping them involved throughout the process ensures they know what's going to happen and when, and are more likely to see that they will still have their jobs but be able to produce much more, making the business more successful.

How Do I Do It?

There are a number of change management models from researchers and journals which help to describe the phases or feelings that people experience when confronted with uncertainty or change. People also react in different ways and so require different management styles to help them deal with the changes constructively. It's worth researching these models and approaches in more detail to find one that resonates with you and your staff. In general, there are some things you can do to make change a successful and positive experience:

- Make sure everyone is aware of the company's strategy and that a change is being considered, such as new technology, new products, or a different company structure, and how this will help the company achieve its targets.

- Hold regular discussions and engagement events with the staff to encourage their ideas and suggestions, as well as to understand their concerns, so you can work out the best way of resolving them.

- Maintain communication throughout, for example, taking staff to see the different technology suppliers so they can try the products out and see how they will work with them in practice. Involving them in the decision-making process will also improve their engagement and enthusiasm for the change.

- Think about the effect the change will have on people's day-to-day lives and talk about it in these terms – they are more likely to be interested in what it means for their salary or the practicalities of what they will do during a working day, than they are about company sales or productivity.

- Speak to other people who have gone through a similar experience; this could be other leaders to find out how they managed the change and what they would do differently, as well as arranging visits for staff to see the technology or processes in operation in another company.

What Are the Benefits and Limitations?

✓ Improve employee engagement and job satisfaction, while also increasing the likelihood of the change being successful.

✓ Encouraging suggestions from staff will often result in a more effective solution.

– There will always be some resistance to change; the aim is to understand the reasons for it and try to address them, so look for people who can champion the change in each area of the business – someone who is respected and can openly discuss issues with people in the area.

Useful Search Terms

- Change management in SMEs.
- Change management models.
- Management or leadership styles.

EQUALITY, DIVERSITY, AND INCLUSION

What Is It?

It means running a company, department, or a team in such a way that all staff feel that they can be themselves, and that the culture of the business is open, attracting people from any background or area of society. A diverse workforce is one that is representative of the wider society and respects the differences people have. Inclusion is simply making a person feel valued and included. The impacts are far reaching and when approached with empathy and commitment, both the business and the staff will benefit significantly. Having a workforce and culture like this will:

- Improve problem-solving – a group of people with different experiences and backgrounds will have different approaches to problems, and as a result will generate more creative solutions. This could mean that a product is designed to work in more situations or is more adaptable because it has been designed by a diverse group of people. This would open a wider potential market for the product and could increase sales. Similarly, having a diverse marketing team would mean that any adverts, press releases, or social media posts are more effective because they can reach and appeal to more of the population, without unknowingly isolating people.

- Improve employee engagement and job satisfaction – staff that feel like their opinions and beliefs are observed and accounted for are more likely to suggest improvements, commit to their role, and feel invested in the success of the company as a whole.

- Reduce staff turnover and attract new talent – people who are respected and fit in well with the culture of the organisation are more likely to stay, and similarly a company which openly demonstrates an inclusive workplace will find it easier to attract new employees, making recruitment more effective, easier, and less time-consuming.

How Do I Do It?

Changing the culture of an organisation doesn't happen overnight and will require commitment and effort from the leadership team; it is also something that is never complete – it requires regular consideration and action, but the benefits will make it worthwhile.

The topic is far reaching and the first step is to approach it with an open mind. Remember that the experiences that have shaped you as a person will be different from everyone else's experiences. It goes further than meeting the legal requirement of not discriminating against the nine protected characteristics, although it is worthwhile reviewing these, then checking how your company not only prevents discrimination but also how it could encourage, accommodate, and improve the working lives of people with protected characteristics. For example, look at gender pay gaps, equal maternity and paternity leave, accommodating leave for various religious celebrations, adding pronouns to email signatures, or fitting hearing aid loops to the offices. It's also worth reviewing any marketing material to check they represent a diverse workforce.

Measure the diversity of your workforce, and check if it is representative of the local community, government statistics are available for this. Create a diversity and inclusion policy to set out how your company will treat everyone fairly and equally, what is expected from all staff, and what the appropriate procedures are for reporting unacceptable behaviour. During this process be sure to discuss it with staff, explaining why you're doing it and ask what they think should be included, or use engagement surveys for a wider view. External training or support is available, make use of this to educate everyone on the policy, but also to raise awareness and educate on individual groups from different cultures, sections of society, and those with different characteristics. Encourage staff to act as champions for diversity and inclusion, or to set up networks celebrating these groups and use them to continually educate people and develop the inclusive culture.

What Are the Benefits and Limitations?

- ✓ Develop an inclusive culture which is more effective and increases business resilience.
- ✓ Improved employee satisfaction, with higher staff retention and easier recruitment.
- ✓ Access new markets and develop improved products and services.
- – Creating a diverse and inclusive workforce will take time, and it may be met with resistance, so make the most of support from external agencies to help with education and commit to the process.

Useful Search Terms

- Diversity and inclusion policies for SMEs.
- Diversity, inclusion, and equality support in *<<location>>*.
- Diversity and inclusion accreditation in *<<location>>*.

EMPLOYEE RETENTION

What Is It?

It is making the working environment attractive to current staff encouraging them to stay and develop their career within your company, rather than looking for jobs elsewhere. As a small manufacturer it can be difficult to balance paying salaries which match other employers in the area with making the business profitable, fortunately there are alternative approaches which make the business a more attractive place to work, such as:

- An employee assistance programme provides benefits such as legal advice, healthcare services, and discounts on shopping and gym memberships. It's common to have this when working for larger companies, but it is also an accessible benefit to provide for employees of smaller businesses. For example, this will give access to support for mental health issues or physiotherapists to help recovery from injuries, meaning that they have less time off work and also feel valued as an employee. Many employee assistance programme providers have subscription models aimed at small companies, making it an affordable option.
- Training and career progression is an important aspect of a role and is one of the reasons an employee looks to leave for another job. People are an important part of the business, and so helping to identify training needs will upskill them, increase their value, and provide more job satisfaction. Similarly, talking through career progressions with employees will show that they're valued, give them a wider variety of experiences, and help them see what their future in the company looks like. Define roles and responsibilities, covered earlier in the chapter, and use key performance indicators for each area, with rewards for meeting targets, to help with motivation and development, see 'Key Performance Indicator' section.
- The working environment is important because it is where the staff spend the majority of their time, making it comfortable and even

enjoyable will improve motivation and set your business apart from competition. Manufacturing environments can be noisy and involve dirty processes, but it's still possible to make these more comfortable by providing quality personal protective equipment, prioritising safety, and looking at the ergonomics of the workplace, such as making tools easily accessible. Providing clean kitchens or break rooms with places where staff can prepare food or have a free hot drink during their break can make a big difference.

- Flexible working arrangements show that a company recognises people have busy lives with different priorities. Establishing methods where people can complete their work at a time that suits them will help make their lives easier and make them more productive. For example, allowing staff to start later and finish earlier to fit in with school times, or having flexible lunch breaks so people can go to the gym or the library will improve their well-being.

How Do I Do It?

Understanding the needs of your staff will help to identify the best approach, talk to them about their concerns or issues, agree to look into solutions, and then discuss the options with them. Use a more general suggestion scheme to help staff anonymously say what they would like to see improved, and this can also help with improvements in other areas of the business too – if the frustrating parts of the job are taken away, it will be more enjoyable and staff are less likely to leave. When staff do decide to leave, exit interviews may be helpful to find out their reasons.

What Are the Benefits and Limitations?

- ✓ Reduced staff turnover, along with a reduction in recruitment time and costs.
- ✓ Improved employee engagement and job satisfaction.
- ✓ There are many options and a lot of them will cost less than pay increases, but they could be more valuable to staff.
- – Some options could cause disruption initially, such as flexible working or increased annual leave, so look at how the work is planned in the areas and adjust this accordingly, succession planning and a skills matrix will help.

Useful Search Terms

- Employee assistance programme for SME.
- Employee retention strategies for SME.

MENTORS

What Is It?

It is an independent person to discuss issues, ideas, or strategies with. For a leader of a smaller manufacturing business, a mentor is someone from a different company who has experience of the challenges and issues that someone in a leadership role faces. Having a mentor is a valuable asset, because it provides someone to talk to, who has been in similar circumstances, and they can pass on their experience and knowledge, which will help with how the business is run, career progression, and work–life balance. Even though every company is different and the details of the issues won't be identical, the process of talking the problems through with someone who isn't directly involved will give a different perspective, and help to formulate the approach to solving them.

Mentors can also be a useful development tool for junior staff to improve their career progression. Where possible, the mentor should be from a different department or outside of the reporting line so the discussions are confidential and separate from any performance reviews. If this isn't possible, the mentor sessions should be held on their own, rather than as part of other development reviews, and the rules or focus of the sessions should be agreed in advance and adhered to, so that they avoid straying into day-to-day work discussions.

How Do I Do It?

A mentor is a long-term relationship so start by thinking what you want to get out of the process, where you and the business need to be in the next few years, and what the issues or challenges you'd like support with; try to separate the short-term problems you're currently facing.

There are many places to find a mentor, and some will be more appropriate than others, depending on what you'd like to address. Here are some suggestions:

- Think about people you've worked with in the past or part of your current network. Are there people you respect and admire in suppliers, customers, trade organisations, or other businesses who may be willing to help.

- Local or national support agencies run mentor schemes, where they can help to match you with someone who has the appropriate experience and knowledge.
- Trade organisations or professional bodies offer mentors, in some cases these help applicants who wish to be members or achieve accreditation, but they are also a good place to network and find potential mentors.

Once you have found a mentor it's important to agree how the sessions will work. For example, how often will you meet, what will be discussed, is there anything off-limits, or are there particular areas to focus on. This will help to make the sessions run more smoothly and maximise the benefit. Once these are agreed, make time for the meetings so that they happen regularly, but also make sure that you have time to prepare for them, consider what will be discussed, and reflect on them afterwards to put any ideas into practice.

What Are the Benefits and Limitations?

- ✓ An independent person to talk to will help to share knowledge and experience, as well as put any problems into perspective and provide a different opinion on the solutions.
- ✓ Improved career progression, networking, and problem-solving for people involved in mentoring.
- – The relationship is personal, and it may take time to find the right mentor, so identifying the aims of having a mentor and agreeing any boundaries for the discussions will help.

Useful Search Terms

- Mentor scheme for SME leaders in <<*location or industry*>>.

WORKFORCE ENGAGEMENT

What Is It?

It is how well employees relate to the company, how much they enjoy their work, and taking steps to understand and improve this. When staff understand the vision, priorities, values, and ethics of a company the day-to-day tasks and requests are put into context and can help to improve productivity. If the values of the staff match those of the business, then they're more likely to engage with the work, make positive contributions, and stay with the company because they'll feel invested in its success.

Taking steps to improve workforce engagement can improve productivity, reduce absenteeism and presenteeism, reduce stress, improve autonomy, increase staff retention, and make the company more attractive to potential employees. These are achieved by being clear about what the company stands for and what it plans to achieve in the future, for example:

- Share the company's strategy, including what it means for the staff, roles, and the company's sites. Knowing where the company is heading will reduce uncertainty, allow employees to prioritise tasks which will move the company towards its goals, and improve job satisfaction.
- Encourage an open and positive culture to provide honest feedback and identify improvements.
- Share the company's values, what is important and why. If the company is developing lower carbon products, sponsoring local community groups, or working with charities, then make this known to the staff, let them know how they can get involved, and embed it into the company's values.
- Allow staff time for special interest groups within the company, where people from different areas of the business with a common interest can meet and plan activities which will educate and share their passions with their colleagues. This could be anything from people who cycle to work, through to people with an interest in cooking, people with similar backgrounds, to people who volunteer for charities.

How Do I Do It?

Start by understanding what people think about the company, what they think about working there, how it's viewed from outside, what they like, and what they don't like. Employee engagement surveys are available, which allow people to anonymously provide feedback; these can be repeated each year to track improvements.

Create a strategy for the company, covered in Chapter 1, along with a statement on the values and behaviours expected from people that work; this is an important step in creating a vision that people can buy into.

Take suggestions and be open to feedback from any member of staff. For example, it may be important to the staff that the company pledges to be net zero by a certain date, engages more with the local community, improves the canteen, publishes gender pay details, or improves the maternity and paternity allowance. While some of these can take time, showing a commitment to making improvements and providing regular updates will build confidence and engagement.

What Are the Benefits and Limitations?

✓ Improved productivity, through aligning people's tasks with the company's strategy.

✓ Higher job satisfaction and reduced stress.

✓ Reduced staff turnover and improved recruitment.

– Culture change takes time, so stick with the process and keep talking with staff to find out what's working, what isn't, and to find out what else can be done, see 'Change Management' section.

Useful Search Terms

• Workforce/employee engagement survey.

• Workforce engagement strategies/examples.

SKILLS MATRIX

What Is It?

It is a document showing the roles in the company, the skills associated with each one, and the level each employee has achieved. This not only improves how training is managed within a team, but also helps with balancing skills across shifts, succession planning, and career progression.

For example, a skills matrix for a welding area would list each employee, the products or types of weld that are required for the job, the welds they are certified to perform, and highlight any which they are required to learn. This would allow the production leader to plan shifts accommodating people's skills, ensuring that production can continue even when people are on leave or if the product mix changes. It would then be used to identify any skills gaps and plan in the training to get the required number of welders approved for each weld type. Finally, it could be used in developmental discussions around probation, pay reviews, or succession planning.

The same template could be applied in other areas of the business, such as assembly, sales, or finance, to ensure the business is resilient in all functions, and that staff understand what is required in their role and how they can develop. See Figure 2.1 for an example.

How Do I Do It?

The outline of a skills matrix is best created by someone who knows the job well, such as a production leader or a team leader. The first step is to create a list of the tasks required in a department, job role, or production cell, and these should be the tasks which are critical to it operating successfully.

Fill in the names of the staff in the area, and include any vacancies so that you get a full picture of the team's requirements. Against each task add the score for the employee, based on whether they can perform the task to the required level or not, or if they aren't required to. In areas where certification is required, such as having achieved a forklift truck licence or having completed a project management training course, filling in the matrix will be straightforward. But in areas where the ability of staff is more subjective, such as knowing the details of a product, providing high-quality customer service, or performing creative processes, then it may be more appropriate to handle this sensitively and keep the matrix private to avoid embarrassing team members, while creating a plan to upskill them.

Review the skills matrix regularly, as part of planning processes as well as development reviews with the team. Make plans to fill any gaps in the team and agree them with the team members to support their progression.

There is a template and example in the resources section of the website.

What Are the Benefits and Limitations?

✓ Clear understanding of the capabilities of the team compared to what's required for successful delivery of the team's objectives.

✓ Allows focused and fact-based development discussions, pay awards, and training identification.

✓ Improves succession planning and team planning.

– The ambition might be to have everyone skilled at every task, but this could be unrealistic, so take time to consider what is essential for the success of the team, and what is optional.

Person	Company induction	Health and safety briefing	Welding certification	Product "A" welding	Product "A" inspection	Product "B" welding	Product "B" inspection	Aftersales support	Sales process
Name 1	Complete 25 Sep 2019	Complete 25 Sep 2019	Last: Jul 2023 Due: Jan 2024	Skilled	Skilled	Skilled	Skilled	Skilled	Skilled
Name 2	Complete 12 Oct 2018	Complete 13 Oct 2018	Last: Mar 2023 Due: Sep 2023	Skilled	Skilled	Required	Required	Development opportunity	Not required
Name 3	Complete 31 Jan 2017	Complete 31 Jan 2017	Not required	Not required	Skilled	Not required	Skilled	Skilled	Development opportunity
Name 4	Complete 25 Feb 2023	Complete 25 Feb 2023	Last: Jul 2023 Due: Jan 2024	Skilled	Skilled	Training required	Training required	Training required	Skilled
Name 5	Complete 2 Jul 2023	Complete 3 Jul 2023	Not required	Not required	Not required	Not required	Not required	Not required	Skilled
Name 6	Due by 5 Nov 2023	Due by 5 Nov 2023	Not required	Not required	Not required	Not required	Not required	Not required	Skilled

FIGURE 2.1   An example of a skills matrix.

Useful Search Terms

- Skills matrix examples.
- Workforce development support in <<*location*>>.

BIBLIOGRAPHY

CIPD. *Equality, diversity and inclusion (EDI) in the workplace.* August 2023. Available at www.cipd.org/ uk/knowledge/factsheets/diversity-factsheet/

Holding, M. *Why we kneel how we rise.* Simon & Schuster, 2022.

Perez, CC. *Invisible women: Data bias in a world designed for men.* Chatto & Windus, 2019.

CHAPTER 3

The Technologies

INDUSTRY 4.0

What Is It?

It is the fourth industrial revolution. The first being steam power and mechanisation, second was electrification and mass production, third was automation in the late 1960s, and the fourth is the use of data and integrating systems to make production more efficient and allow the creation of new products or services. The technologies which fall under the Industry 4.0 term are:

- Additive manufacturing or 3D printing.
- Augmented reality (AR), virtual reality (VR), extended reality (XR), or mixed reality (MR).
- Big data and analytics.
- Artificial intelligence (AI).
- Data and systems integration, or more generally, software solutions.
- Industrial cyber security.

DOI: 10.1201/9781032642215-4

- Industrial internet of things (IIoT).
- Mobile devices and wearable technology.
- Robotics and process control automation.

These are very broad descriptors covering a number of technologies, which often won't be implemented on their own. The most appropriate for manufacturing companies are covered in the later chapters of this book.

How Do I Do It?

The key thread that runs through the idea of Industry 4.0 is the use and sharing of data. Look for areas in your business where data or information is difficult to access, where it's duplicated, or where people don't have easy access to the information that would make their jobs simpler. Common examples are piles of paperwork, using carbon paper to generate multiple copies, typing information from one system into another, or not understanding costs and profitability of different products.

Various software systems could help alleviate these issues, but Industry 4.0 doesn't just cover software. Machines running on their own often gather data which isn't used, such as the number of parts processed, when the last service took place, oil levels, or key process parameters. Look on the machine manufacturer's website to see if this data is accessible, larger companies will have a dedicated page for their Industry 4.0 services which will give you an idea of what's possible.

Use tools such as process mapping or the technology strategy to identify issues in your company which need resolving as a priority, then research technologies or suppliers which can provide a solution – technology pull rather than technology push.

What Are the Benefits and Limitations?

- ✓ Improved productivity.
- ✓ Improved employee autonomy and job satisfaction.
- ✓ Unlocking hidden production capacity or new products and services.
- – Industry 4.0 is a broad term, you need to identify the issues and select a particular technology which will address these issues.

Useful Search Terms

- *<<Equipment supplier name>>* Industry 4.0.
- Automate *<<production process or office task>>* in *<<industry>>*.
- *<<Industry>>* trade organisation exhibition *<<country or location>>*.

ADDITIVE MANUFACTURING (AM) OR 3D PRINTING

What Is It?

It is the creation of physical products or models by adding material, usually layer by layer, rather than removing material as with traditional manufacturing techniques such as milling or turning. By adding material where it's needed it's possible to make shapes and profiles which are impossible to make with other manufacturing techniques, so additive manufacturing (AM) opens a range of opportunities to a company.

There are thousands of materials available for AM, from plastics, metals, composites, through to chocolate or concrete, it's worth investigating what's available in your industry. Similarly, there are a huge number of machine manufacturers ranging in price from £100 to £100,000s and with a large number of different types of processes too, it is important to understand your needs and find an appropriate system.

When the technology first emerged it was often just used to create prototypes, and while this is still a common use case, AM can be used to create finished components of extremely high quality and which outperform traditional components due to the design opportunities. For example, only putting material where it's needed can reduce component weight, complex internal geometries can allow optimal fluid flow, and not needing to produce dies or patterns can mean lower production volumes are viable and with higher levels of customisation.

How Do I Do It?

The process starts with a digital model on a computer-aided design (CAD) software package, a slicing software programme is then used to split this up into layers, and in some cases support structures need to be added where material will overhang during the build. The layer thickness is determined by the printing process which will be used – thicker layers will generally be quicker but have a rougher surface finish, whereas thinner layers will be slower but allow more fine details in the model and a smoother finish. Once the CAD model has been prepared it is sent to the machine to be printed. When the build has finished the physical part can be removed from the machine and will often need post-processing, which involves removing the support structures, cleaning out any residual material left in and around the part, and finishing with a polishing process, painting, or in some cases curing or sintering to achieve the desired material properties.

Local 3D printing bureaus or research centres will be able to guide you through the process of selecting which material and machine type you need, as well as allowing you to produce components for performance testing, without investing in your own machine.

What Are the Benefits and Limitations?

✓ Huge range of materials and processes available.

✓ Quickly produce multiple design options for assessment.

✓ Design freedom allows performance improvements.

✓ Parts can be produced where they're needed, avoiding shipping time and costs.

– Knowledge and experience of the processes is required, look for local 3D printing bureaus or suppliers, and see 'Where to go for Technical Support' section.

– Material validation can take time in highly regulated industries, ensure this is accounted for in the plan and agree the testing requirements in advance.

– The process can be slow (build times measured in hours or days) making it unviable for simple parts, ask for demonstrations by equipment suppliers or use bureaus to test processes before investing in your own machine.

Useful Search Terms

• Additive manufacturing in <<*industry*>> or <<*material*>>.

• 3D printing bureau in <<*location*>>.

TYPES OF ADDITIVE MANUFACTURING OR 3D PRINTING PROCESSES

There are many different types of additive manufacturing processes, which are grouped into seven categories, as defined by the American

Society for Testing and Materials and the International Organization for Standardization in ISO/ASTM 52900:2021[1]. There is a lot of jargon and each manufacturer may use different terms for their processes, which adds to the names and acronyms, so the list below aims to summarise these allowing you to identify which process type may be most suitable for your use and material type.

Material Extrusion

A moveable head pushes material through a heater and then a nozzle to deposit it accurately where it's required. As the nozzle moves away the deposited material solidifies forming a solid structure, and this is repeated layer by layer until the part is complete. Domestic 3D printing systems are usually material extrusion, and so provide a low-cost introduction to the technology, but there are also more advanced systems available for production use and creating finished products.

Material types: metals, plastics, composites, and almost anything else that can be extruded, such as chocolate or concrete.
Uses: finished parts, prototypes, bespoke jigs and fixtures, casting patterns, casings.

Directed Energy Deposition

A moveable nozzle deposits the build material, as powder or wire feed, where it is needed, and an energy source melts the material to fix it in place. The energy source could be a weld head, electron beam, or laser; with the nozzle being controlled by a 5-axis machine or robot. This process can be applied to an existing component, or the model can be built up from scratch. Machining or finishing processes are usually required due to the surface finish and accuracy of the material deposition.

Material types: usually just metals, occasionally plastics.
Uses: repairing components which are long lead time or expensive by adding material just where it's needed, or for very large or low-volume components.

Powder Bed Fusion

The machine spreads a thin layer of powder material across the build plate, before a laser or electron beam melts the areas which need to be joined together. The machine then lowers the build plate slightly, before adding another thin layer of powder, and melting the areas needed for that layer. This is repeated until the model is complete. The entire block of powder is removed from the machine, and the model has to be extracted from this in the post-processing operation. Metallic powders can be processed in a vacuum to improve the mechanical properties.

Material types: metals, plastics.
Uses: finished structural parts, low-volume parts, parts requiring particular material properties or specific alloys.

Binder Jetting

This process deposits the build material as a powder on the first layer, followed by a second layer of a binder material which acts as an adhesive. This is applied by a print head similar to an inkjet printer. The adhesive is only placed where it is needed for the model, and then the next layer of powder is added on top, followed by another adhesive layer. This is repeated until the model is complete, and it can be removed from the machine. The areas of powder which haven't been bound together by the adhesive are removed to reveal the model.

Material types: metals, plastics, and ceramics.
Uses: non-structural parts as the binder material can affect the strength, or non-functional parts such as casting moulds or cores, and product prototypes.

Material Jetting

Small drops of material are deposited, one by one, onto the build area where they solidify. This is similar to an inkjet printer, but the build area is lowered slightly after each layer, allowing the model to be built up. The finished models may need curing with heat or light to harden them.

Material types: Wax or special polymers.
Uses: full colour medical models, prototypes, casting patterns.

Sheet Lamination

Sheets of material are added and fused together to form the part. In some cases the sheets have been precut into profiles and built up, or the sheets can be fused in specific areas and the unwanted material machined away to leave the part. Metal sheets are fused by ultrasonic or laser welding, whereas paper is joined using an adhesive.

Material types: Thin sheet metal, plastic, paper.
Uses: prototypes and multi-material models.

Vat Polymerisation

A container holds liquid resin and the build platform, while a light source cures the resin, solidifying the required areas on the first layer. The platform moves down slightly before the process is repeated on the second layer, bonding it with the first. Layer by layer the model is built up, and once complete it is removed, before being cured to prevent degradation in sunlight.

Material types: Curable polymers.
Uses: prototypes, casting patterns, small-scale models, or models with intricate features.

ARTIFICIAL INTELLIGENCE (AI) AND MACHINE LEARNING (ML)

What Is It?

It is using computer software in a way which mimics how the human brain works in order to solve complex problems. AI takes the fact that computers can process very large amounts of data very quickly and uses it to make decisions based on a set of defined rules. ML is a subset of AI, and this uses the approach to problem-solving that humans normally take in order to continually learn and improve the model. The terms AI and ML are often used interchangeably, the rest of this section will use AI.

For example, one way AI can be used in a factory is preventative maintenance, where data from a machine is fed into an AI system. This could include temperature, vibration, running speeds, or any number of process parameters which are important to how the machine operates, see also Industrial Internet of Things (IIoT) and key process variables (KPVs) covered later in the chapter. An AI model could learn how these parameters vary during normal production, and then send an alert when they stray from the norm. This is a task which a person could do by plotting charts of tool speed during different machine cycles and then identifying the optimum range of speeds for each, but this would take a significant amount of time and the AI model has the advantage that it will spot trends and correlations which a person may miss. A similar approach could be applied to complex order patterns to help with demand forecasting in a business. Once the model is defined it is relatively easy to add new machines or data sets from different customers to get additional benefits.

Large language models (LLMs) are a type of AI which use vast amounts of data to train a system in order to answer questions in natural language. AI chatbots are based on LLMs, and can be used to create marketing content, proofread documents, create quotes, summarise meetings, and research topics. Chatbots are now starting to be embedded into search engines to provide a more personalised experience.

How Do I Do It?

The simplest way is to experiment with AI chatbots to help with generating ideas, learning about new topics, or suggesting ideas for the next company newsletter or marketing campaign.

Alternatively, try software which has the functionality built in, such as some enterprise resource planning (ERP) systems, specific modules of an ERP system if it's needed for a particular task such as production planning or stock management, or machine monitoring services using low-cost sensors and pre-made software ('Industrial Internet of Things' section). Similarly, chatbots are commonplace on websites now. These are often powered by AI and are off-the-shelf systems which will need an element of training on your products and services.

For more bespoke or complex tasks a number of services are available which provide the building blocks of an AI model and allow you to create your own. If you have the skills in your company and an unusual use case this maybe a good option. Alternatively, look for a software developer with skills in AI or ML who could do this for you.

Whichever approach is taken it's recommended that you have a clear set of requirements and establish boundaries for the model to ensure you know it is fit for purpose. Before using the model to make decisions, it's best practice to check that the outputs are in line with what you would expect, and you should be able to interrogate the model to establish why a particular answer was reached.

What Are the Benefits and Limitations?

✓ Large amounts of data can be processed and analysed automatically, spotting trends or correlations between different data sets.

✓ Automates tasks which would take a person a very long time to complete.

✓ Chatbots can quickly summarise topics or create marketing content.

– Custom systems need access to large amount of training data, see 'Big Data' section.

– The rules the model use need to be transparent so the answers can be trusted, ensure this is included in the requirements from the start of the project.

Useful Search Terms

• Prompt engineering guide.

• Guide to using AI for <<*task*>>. For example, "guide to using AI for creating marketing content".

• AI module or plugin for <<*software package*>>.

• AI providers in <<*industry*>>.

• AI software developers in <<*location*>>.

BIG DATA

What Is It?

It is the process of collecting, processing, and analysing vast amounts of data from a number of sources in order to improve how the business operates. This is probably data that already exists in your company, for example, you could bring together all the order history from all customers, with supplier delivery information, production times, quality control results, and shift pattern information. With all that information you could start to identify areas for improvement or areas which work particularly well. While this would be technically possible if all these records were on paper, it wouldn't be feasible and it would be easy to miss links and connections between data sets. The advent of faster computer processors and connected software systems make this task much more manageable and more effective, because the analysis tools offer more advanced techniques to bring out trends and correlations.

As an example, with the data sets mentioned above, the analysis might highlight that product quality is higher when material from a certain supplier is used on a certain machine, but not on others, allowing you to investigate the causes of this and make adjustments so the higher quality is achieved on all the machines.

Data lakes and data warehouse are also terms associated with big data. A data lake is all the information in a company, but in an unstructured or different format, so while the data is there it would need to be processed before it could be analysed. A data warehouse is the same set of data but one which is stored in a cleaned state, so it can be used effectively and with minimal processing. Data lakes and warehouses are usually required to train AI models, see 'Artificial Intelligence' section.

How Do I Do It?

All the data you plan to use needs to be in an electronic format, rather than paper-based. For example, this means using a customer relationship management (CRM) software to store all the information about your customers and what they've ordered, or an enterprise resource planning (ERP) system could be used to store more of the company's information in one place. The data needs to be accessible or exported to a single place where it can be accessed by the analysis software, and then it needs to be cleaned and processed so that it's all in the correct format. When the data is ready to be analysed, start with different theories or hypotheses and use data analysis techniques to test if these are correct or not, or alternatively it's possible to use pre-built functions to automatically check the data for correlations or patterns which you may not be aware of.

What Are the Benefits and Limitations?

✓ Make use of the data you already have, to identify improvements.

✓ Improve demand forecasting or production planning by understanding trends in your business.

✓ Empower employees to use data and make data-driven decisions.

– Data is often in siloes in different software applications making it difficult to get started, use a software architecture diagram to understand where data is stored and how it can be improved ('System Architecture Diagram' section).

– Data analytics skills may not exist in the business, however, free training is available online from a number of providers which will act as a good introduction..

Useful Search Terms

- Extract/analyse data from <<*software package or cloud service*>>.
- Data analysis skills/techniques in manufacturing.
- Capture/extract data from <<*machine make and model*>>.

AUTOMATION

What Is It?

It is using any type of machine or device to perform a process without, or with reduced, intervention from a person. In manufacturing it is usually a purpose-built, self-operating machine that performs a repetitive task which was previously done manually.

The range of automation available is vast, and it can be tempting to think of large robots assembling cars or complex production lines making thousands of products a minute, and then decide that automation is out of reach for a small manufacturer. It can also be a concern for operators on the shop floor who may expect that once tasks are automated, they will be made redundant. However, this is rarely the case. Introducing a simple machine to add labels onto wires, for example, would be low cost, but would mean a skilled technician is spending more of their time performing complex tasks that are more interesting and more profitable, rather than spending their time labelling. As a result, their job is more fulfilling and they can produce more in a shift.

How Do I Do It?

Traditionally companies would look to bring automation in for the "dull, dangerous, or dirty" tasks, and while this mantra is still appropriate, it's also worth looking at the entire manufacturing facility to identify bottlenecks, areas of poor quality, or tasks that are difficult to recruit for, as opportunities for implementing automation.

Firstly, gather data and identify current issues that affect the business. Then, prioritise these and select the one which will have the most impact.

Write down your requirements for the process and include things such as how many products does it need to process, how many product variants are there, what size are they, and any expected changes in future production rates see 'Requirements Capture – Hardware'.

Investigate solutions and discuss your requirements with suppliers – this could be a bespoke system created by an automation integrator, or an off-the-shelf solution. Use the requirements document to objectively compare the proposals and select the one which is the best fit for your business.

Consult and involve the staff from the area throughout the process to ensure that they understand why you are looking to automate some of their tasks, and to ensure you find a solution they'll use and which will be effective.

What Are the Benefits and Limitations?

✓ Improved processing time, product quality, and productivity.

✓ Higher staff engagement and improved job satisfaction.

✓ Increased company profile.

– Some tasks aren't suitable for automation, so the process needs to be designed around the manual processes, use a requirements document, a process map, or a process input/output diagram to describe this to any potential suppliers.

– Involving staff late in the process can result in underused equipment, get their feedback at the start of the project and include them throughout to.

Useful Search Terms

- Automation in <<*industry*>>.
- Machine to perform <<*task*>>.
- <<*Industry*>> integrators in <<*location*>>. For example, "food and drink industry automation integrators in Yorkshire".

ROBOTICS

What Is It?

It is a type of automation which involves the use of a machine, usually a mechanical arm which can move in three or more directions, used to complete tasks faster and more efficiently than doing it manually. Robotics is applied when a flexible approach is needed, such as coping with several different product types, or when a purpose-built machine isn't available.

The range of robots available is increasing all the time, from small robots costing less than £10,000 through to large robots which are capable of lifting over a tonne; and as such the likelihood of finding a robot suitable for a particular application at an agreeable cost is increasing. To add to this, many robot suppliers offer lease options or robotics-as-a-service solutions to lower the barriers to entry. The common types of robots are:

- Industrial robots – used for jobs which require high speeds, heavy tools or products, or operate in harsh environments. They require safety cages or additional safety systems, and often need specialist programming skills.

- Collaborative robots (cobots) – designed to work safely in the same space as people, without the need for safety barriers, but a thorough risk assessment is required to enable this. Cobots can be easily programmed, moved, and quickly repurposed to perform a different task. They are often used to assist an operator with product assembly, packing, loading and unloading machines, welding, or palletising products.

- Delta robots – usually consist of three or four arms connected to a base, and are designed to be extremely fast and precise. They are often used in large-scale food production, to move delicate items into boxes, for example.

- Selective compliance articulated robot arm (SCARA) – a three-axis robot with one of the axes being complaint. They are often used for pick and place or sorting tasks.

- Autonomous mobile robot (AMR) – used to automatically deliver components or products to different areas of a factory or warehouse ('Warehouse Automation section).

How Do I Do It?

See the 'Automation' section for the initial steps, as there may be a solution to the problem which uses automation, rather than robotics, and it will also help to capture your requirements allowing any suppliers or integrators to create a proposal most suited to your needs. If robotics looks like the most viable option, then consider these areas when developing your solution:

- Carefully design the infeed and outfeed system, making sure the loading and unloading area or the surrounding workspace is efficient and comfortable for the operator.
- Consider the end effectors, or end of arm tooling, which is how the robot interacts with the part. Examples are vacuum grabbers, physical grippers, a paint gun, or a polishing head.
- Check the accuracy, speed, and payload are appropriate as these vary with the robot's position.
- A thorough risk assessment is mandatory to ensure it will operate safely.

What Are the Benefits and Limitations?

✓ Increased production capacity, through unsupervised operation.

✓ Very repeatable when performing tasks.

– In most cases cells are bespoke and require specialist integration (less so with cobots), plan for this in the requirements document, and use a skills matrix (see 'Skills Matrix' section) to develop the in-house skills like programming and maintenance.

Useful Search Terms

- Robotics in <<*industry*>>.
- Robotic <<*task*>> in <<*production type*>>. For example, "robotic welding in jobbing shop".

VISION SYSTEMS AND MACHINE VISION

What Is It?

It is using sensors to allow a machine or software to process a component based on its appearance. This could be using a laser scanner to detect barcodes passing it on a conveyor belt or using a camera input to allow a robot to detect the orientation of components. The sensor is part of a larger system, both in terms of the machine vision itself but also what to do with the information it gathers, how this is used by the machine or software is equally important. For example, adding a vision system to a conveyor belt in a warehouse would require the following elements:

- A vision system to detect barcodes or QR codes on boxes as they pass the sensor.

- A system to take the information from the vision system and decode it, such as turning the barcode into a product identifier.
- Software or hardware to take this information and decide what to do; it could be to check the product is in the correct place or to instruct the conveyor system where to send the product.

This is similar to 3D scanning (see '3D scanning' section), which is used for component inspection or factory scanning.

How Do I Do It?

The most important part is to decide on the requirements of the system before discussing with potential suppliers so that you find a solution that suits your business. This could include:

- What information needs to be collected by the sensor.
- How quickly the information needs to be read – fast moving parts on a conveyor system will need a different solution to stationary parts waiting to be loaded into a machine.
- What software or hardware the sensing system will need to interact with, and what format the data needs to be in.
- The number of parts or products to be processed in a given time period.
- The number of variations in products, such as the surface material, different colours, or more reflective surfaces which can affect how well products can be scanned.
- The environment where the scanning will take place, in particular the lighting and if this is consistent from overhead lights, or variable from sunlight coming through the window.

What Are the Benefits and Limitations?

- ✓ Reduced operator involvement, allowing them to focus on more skilled tasks.
- ✓ Faster and more accurate processing compared to manual checks.
- ✓ Systems are scalable so can be installed step by step.
- – Additional systems will be required to process and act on the data collected, so ensure these are accounted for when budgeting and scoping the full solution.
- – Conveyor systems will probably need a higher volume of parts to justify the cost.

Useful Search Terms

- Conveyor system with barcode scanning systems in <<*industry*>>.
- Automated vision system for <<*manufacturing task*>>.

WAREHOUSE AUTOMATION

What Is It?

It is using machines or systems to automatically process parts or products in a warehouse. This is closely linked to stock management systems, for the software elements see 'Stock or Inventory Management' section. In a warehouse, automation can be retrofitted to cover some individual tasks allowing operators to work more efficiently and process more products, or the warehouse can be set up from the start to operate autonomously with operators just processing the parts to add or retrieve them from the system. Common uses include:

- Carousel storage to make use of the height of a building by installing much taller storage systems, with an automatic retrieval mechanism to deliver the appropriate shelf to the operator. These can operate as a standalone system or they can integrate with other stock management software solutions.

- Autonomous mobile robots (AMRs) are used to carry items around a warehouse and deliver them to where they're required. Some systems run on predetermined routes; others are equipped with sensors to allow them to navigate a warehouse without planned routes and are safe enough to operate in the same area as people.

- Automated retrieval systems are used to make better use of warehouse space by removing the need for forklift access. The racks can be much closer together because the mechanism collects items from a shelf and delivers it to the operator, which also makes more use of vertical space. More complex systems don't have a space between the shelves and stack the products vertically, a number of robots on the top of the shelves working together to remove boxes and retrieve the required item, allowing much more stock can be held in a smaller warehouse area.

- Assisted pick and pack systems are devices used to instruct staff which shelf the product is on, and sometimes they provide the most efficient route through the warehouse to collect a full list of products for an order. These systems use barcodes or QR codes and scanners to quickly input product or location information into the controlling software.

- Automated picking systems can take a full list of products from one order and retrieve them from the various storage locations around the warehouse, then deliver them to an operator for packing.

How Do I Do It?

For the more autonomous systems it's important to understand the process flow of how products enter and leave your warehouse, and what tasks the staff currently do. Use a process map to understand this, discuss with staff what improvements could be made, and formalise this before deciding on the requirements of the system. Select one area to trial the system. A lot of systems can start with a small installation to prove the concept and then add more at a later date. There are a number of providers so shop around and look for one which shares data easily with any current software system you use.

What Are the Benefits and Limitations?

- ✓ Increased storage capacity and improved staff efficiency.
- ✓ Many systems are modular and can start with a small installation to prove the concept.
- ✓ An existing stock control system isn't always necessary, some systems can be standalone.
- – Automated systems are more suited to high-volume processing, but for low-volume businesses storage systems like carousels are appropriate.
- – Complex systems will have a high initial cost, so investigate a number of suppliers and consider the business case ('Business Case' section) to ensure the project provides value for money.

Useful Search Terms

- <<Automation type>> suppliers in <<location>>.
- Supply chain/warehouse automation exhibition in <<location>>.

CYBERSECURITY

What Is It?

It is taking action to make sure your business is protected against the risks of cybercrime. It involves the people and processes in the business as well as the computer equipment and software solutions used. The impact of a cyberattack can be extremely costly and time consuming to a business, so it's worth taking steps to avoid falling victim. Cyberattacks can take a number of forms,[2] both targeted and untargeted, including:

- Phishing is sending emails to a large number of people often tricking them into providing sensitive information by appearing to come from a trusted sender, such as a bank or a supplier. Spear-phishing is the targeted version where the attacker selects particular people who may provide some or all of the information they need to access a system.

- Ransomware is used once an attacker has pieced together enough information about the company in order to hold it to ransom, often they understand the computer systems in use and can freeze or delete the important data until the ransom is paid.

- Distributed denial of service (DDOS) attacks attempt to overload a company's systems by bombarding it with requests. This could be a website or computer system, and the aim is to disrupt the operation of the company by using all the bandwidth or network capacity.

How Do I Do It?

Computer and software systems can be a complex network and it can be difficult to have a complete understanding or oversight of how everything works together, making protecting it seem even more of a challenge. Support is available online from trusted agencies such as the National Cyber Security Centre in the UK, more locally, having a discussion with your IT service providers is a good place to start. It's also worth taking these steps:

- Identify any information which is critical to the business running correctly, such as contact details, documents, or drawings, and ensure they are regularly backed up.

- Plan what you would do in the event of an attack, which customers or suppliers would you need to inform and who would be involved.

- Identify any critical equipment and look at how this can be protected, discuss with your IT providers about making your networks resilient and implementing security protocols such as encryption, two-factor authentication, and virtual private networks.

- Test the systems and practice the plans you've put in place, like running a fire drill, to make sure they work effectively.

What Are the Benefits and Limitations?

- ✓ Protect your company, data, and employees from online threats.

- ✓ Be more attractive to suppliers and customers knowing their data is safe.

- – A complex topic with specialist skills required, but external support is available.

Useful Search Terms

- Cybersecurity support in <<*industry*>> or <<*local area*>>.

- Data protection in small businesses.

- Network resilience techniques.

ENTERPRISE RESOURCE PLANNING (ERP) SOFTWARE

What Is It?

It is software used to manage the data and processes for the entire business. ERP packages are often built up of a series of different modules, depending on what your company needs and how it operates. More information about the individual modules, such as customer relationship management (CRM) or production planning, can be found on the following sections, and while these modules can be used independently and from different providers, in some cases it makes more sense to have a single software solution to do everything.

There are many ERP solutions available, often they have been made specifically for a certain industry, which makes the setup process much simpler and it's more likely to suit how your business operates. For example, an ERP system designed for the brewery industry will have specific elements suited to brewing such as managing the range of ingredients required, recipe storage and management, customer order tracking, and e-commerce integration. Whereas a system designed for the uPVC door industry would allow website integration for customers to design their own products, automated quoting based on material costs, automated bill of materials (BOM) creation, and production planning with the correct method of manufacture included. Alternatively, a company making bespoke welded products will need to look for a supplier suited to them, which allows functionality such as flexibility in BOM, variable methods of manufacture, customisable equipment, and staff skills set up; in this case there are cross-industry options available.

How Do I Do It?

The most important consideration is that the software needs to help your business operate more effectively, and it should fit to how you work, rather than making large changes to your procedures just to fit in with how the software works. To achieve this, the first step is to understand the requirements ('Requirements Capture – Software' section) of the system – which areas of the business do you want it to cover and what tasks do you want it to do. Using process maps ('Process Map' section) and user stories ('User Stories' section) are good methods of explaining this to potential providers. Once the requirements are understood, start to research potential suppliers, and discuss what their system offers, how many of your requirements can be achieved, ask for examples in similar businesses, and discuss any likely future requirements. Once you have a number of proposals, compare them to your original requirements and select the best fit. It's important to allocate people's time to spend on this investigation stage as well as the implementation stage, because your business will be reliant on this working well.

Many companies already use a finance package, and a key consideration is how easily data can be shared between the ERP system and the finance package to reduce manual copying and pasting. Finance packages often have integration stores or approved partners on their website to give a starting point, or look for application programming interface (API) functionality which allows a software developer to create an automatic data connection between the software packages.

What Are the Benefits and Limitations?

- ✓ Reduced time processing information allowing staff to focus on value-added tasks.
- ✓ Information is easily accessible by people who need it.
- ✓ Enables a business to grow by automating data processing tasks.

- Can be complex and time consuming to set up, the project leader needs to be given the time and resources to do it correctly.
- Changing to a different ERP provider can be a difficult decision because all the existing data may not be transferrable to the new system, in this case capturing the requirements and prioritising the data that is critical to the business are important steps.

Useful Search Terms

- ERP solution/provider for <<*industry*>>.
- ERP solution for <<*product type or manufacturing type*>>. For example, "ERP solution for complex customer products" or "ERP for jobbing shop production".
- ERP integration into <<*finance package*>>.

CUSTOMER RELATIONSHIP MANAGEMENT

What Is It?

It is software or a software module used to store and process all information related to customers. This would include information like contact information, logs of any meetings/phone calls/emails between the sales team and the customer, previous order history, and marketing preferences. With this data stored in a central area, firstly it allows the sales team to operate more efficiently because they have quick access to relevant information and they can cover for colleagues because information isn't stored on individual computers. Secondly it allows analysis of the information in order to improve service. This could include alerts when a customer hasn't ordered for a certain amount of time and needs contacting, or identifying trends in order patterns which allows the creation of new products or sales strategies to gain more orders in quieter periods.

How Do I Do It?

For smaller companies there are many free, or low cost, CRM solutions available. This is a great starting point for a young company, as it would allow sales staff to focus on customer relationships and selling products, rather than paperwork and admin tasks, especially if the information is stored on the cloud, allowing them to access it from anywhere on any device. For larger companies which may already have existing software solutions, it's worth checking first if the current software providers have a CRM module, to allow easy data sharing between areas of the business. Understanding what you need the software to do by capturing your requirements is an important step, to ensure that the software will allow you to work in a way that suits your company, that it stores the information you need and in the right format, allows analysis and reporting of this data, and also easily shares the data with other software systems as required without downloading files or manually copying and pasting information.

What Are the Benefits and Limitations?

- ✓ Less time managing paperwork.
- ✓ Increased understanding of customer behaviour through data analysis.
- ✓ A good introduction to digital technology.
- – Often this is the first software solution a company implements; it can be difficult to decide which data to collect and how, use the requirement capture tools to help with this.
- – If software hasn't been used by a company before then there can be some resistance from staff, a particular focus needs to be put on making sure they understand how it will help them do their job and ensure training is planned properly.

Useful Search Terms

- Low-cost CRM in <<*industry*>>.
- CRM solution to integrate with <<*existing software solution*>>.

CUSTOMER PORTALS

What Is It?

It is an area of a website where customers can access information about the status of their order, place new orders, make payments, or customise the products or services to suit them. In its simplest form it could be a website that a customer uses to send in a new order, and it means that the office team always receive the order details in the same format, making processing much easier, compared to checking emails, voicemails, or taking notes while on the phone.

When linked with other systems the benefit to the customer increases and helps to provide them with information automatically, without the office team having to find the information manually. Linking a customer portal with a shop floor data collection system ('Shop Floor Data Capture' section) or an order management system ('Order Tracking' section) would allow them to get accurate updates on where their product is and when they can expect to receive it. Compared to them ringing or emailing a request into the office and somebody having to physically find the order on the shop floor before replying, this is much more efficient and provides an improved level of service over competitors.

Another example would be linking the portal to a CAD package ('Computer Aided Design' section) where design rules have been created to automatically generate designs based on certain criteria. Linking a customer portal to this would mean the customer could input their requirements on a website, then instantly see a model or a drawing of their product, as well as receive a quote, without having to discuss it with the sales team. Car configurators on car manufacturers' websites are a good example of this tool, you can pick the trim, colour, engine type, wheel style, and numerous other options to help you decide what to order as well as see how much it will cost.

How Do I Do It?

Have a look at the information you currently use, and the common information or requests that your customers send to you, and discuss these with the office staff. Through these discussions understand what takes more of their time, and which cause frustration or the most disruption to their day. Process maps ('Process Map' section) or user stories ('User Stories' section) are a good method of capturing these, and form the basis for the requirements of the system ('Requirements Capture – Software' section). Add to this any services which your customers may find useful, or which would differentiate you from the competition.

Once you understand your requirements you can look for providers. This could be addons to services you already use, such as e-commerce, order management systems, and shop floor data collection systems. If you don't use any systems like this there are standalone services, or it may require a custom-built solution with a software developer. Having a bespoke solution created sounds like it will be an expensive option but it can be a cost-effective approach.

What Are the Benefits and Limitations?

- ✓ Increased customer satisfaction while lowering office staff involvement.
- ✓ Provides data on customer orders in a consistent format allowing further analysis.
- – Other systems may be required to automatically provide data, investigate these as part of the initial research, and use a business case ('Business Case' section) to evaluate if it will provide value for money.

Useful Search Terms

- Customer/client portal for manufacturer in <<*industry*>>.
- Software developer in <<*location*>>.
- Customer portal addon for <<*current software in use for order tracking or CAD*>>.

DATA DASHBOARDS AND BUSINESS INTELLIGENCE SOFTWARE

What Is It?

Data dashboards take data from different sources and display relevant analysis where it's needed. Business intelligence (BI) software helps the company to perform these tasks. Ideally the system should be set up to perform the data automatically, but the important element initially is giving people information when they need it. This is closely related to key performance indicators, see Chapter 1, one company could have a number of different dashboards:

- A large screen on the shop floor showing the current production plan, along with performance against current metrics, such as number of products produced this shift, percentage of right first time, and progress towards the monthly bonus pool target.
- A display in the sales office showing number of sales achieved, trends in sales data, a measure of production capacity available for new orders, and current lead times.
- A webpage the leadership team use to monitor the key metrics from each department, as well as energy use and financial measures

from the company, in order to gauge performance and inform decision-making.

How Do I Do It?

It's possible to do this manually by updating spreadsheets and using BI software to analyse and display the data in charts or other accessible formats. This approach is useful when starting to use dashboards, as it's important to understand where the data comes from and what's helpful to people in different areas. Once a shift is complete the number of orders produced, or number of sales made can be added to the spreadsheet, so that the dashboard updates the display. The data can be in different locations, and the BI software can be set up to understand the relationships between the data sets and display the analysis accordingly.

Alternatively, if software is already in use to track things like production, sales, finances, or energy use, then look to automatically share the data with the BI software. It maybe that the software has the functionality to display analysis and metrics on a screen without using BI software, or in some cases there are plugins or partner software solutions which can do this, alternatively an application programming interface (API) can be used to securely share data between software providers.

What Are the Benefits and Limitations?

- ✓ Provides relevant information to staff when they need it, without having to look for it or perform their own analysis.
- ✓ Combines data from different sources to provide more insights into how the business is operating.
- ✓ Makes use of data already collected but is stored and not used.
- ✓ Free and low-cost BI solutions are available.
- – Incorrect data or out of context analysis can be misleading, ensure everyone understands what the dashboards show and what they're intended to be used for.

Useful Search Terms

- Automatically export data from <<*software package*>>.
- Free or low-cost BI software.
- Introduction to data analysis training.

FINANCE SOFTWARE

What Is It?

It is software used to manage the cash and accounting elements of a business. It is often one of the first software platforms to be introduced into a business, as it's important to ensure that the correct information is used by the finance leader or the accountant. The software will be used to manage invoices, purchase orders, tax, payments, as well as providing reporting tools to analyse the performance of the business. Many finance packages link to bank accounts and operate in the cloud so that the data is up to date and can be accessed everywhere, on a range of devices, by the appropriate people involved in running the business.

Basic finance packages can make the financial reporting more straight-forward, particularly for a young business, allowing the leaders to concen-trate on growth. As companies get larger the finance packages offer more services which may be beneficial, such as stock control, payroll, or integra-tion with e-commerce websites. These will be subject to higher monthly fees but will provide benefits to the company without having to implement a standalone module or a full enterprise resource planning (ERP) system ('Enterprise Resource Planning' section).

How Do I Do It?

The selection of a finance package is an important consideration as it often has a bearing on what software can be used in the future – it's easier to export data and automatically share information to other programmes with some finance packages than others. This is very dependent on the type of business, so understanding your requirements for a basic finance package now is critical, but having an idea of what you might want to use it for in the future is almost as important. When looking at options, see what services they offer to larger companies in your sector, as well as the partner or integrations they offer and demonstrate on their website. If the software can use application programming interfaces (API) in order to share data with other programs, this will make it easier for you to use other service providers for different modules in the future, without being tied to just using the finance software or approved partners. Discussing options with your accountant is also a good option as they'll likely have experience of different providers to help you decide.

Once a finance package has been implemented, it's not impossible to change to a different provider, the data can be exported and imported to the new service, but this will take some time and planning to ensure continuity. Compile your requirements ('Requirements Capture – Software' section) and assess the different packages against these, accounting for the switch over time and effort as part of the decision-making process.

What Are the Benefits and Limitations?

✓ Accurate control of company finances, with up-to-date visibility of cash flow and other indicators.

✓ Finance packages often have additional modules which can be beneficial, such as stock control or payroll.

✓ Simpler reporting for tax or other regulatory purposes.

– Data can be difficult to access from other software solutions, so investigate this when choosing a supplier and use a software architecture diagram ('Software Architecture Diagram' section) to show what information needs to be shared.

– Switching to a new finance package can be perceived as difficult, but capturing requirements and deciding which data are critical to transfer can make this easier.

Useful Search Terms

- Finance software for SME manufacturer in <<*industry*>>.

- Export data from <<*finance package*>> to <<*third party software*>>.

- API/software marketplace for <<*finance package*>>.

LOGISTICS PLANNING

What Is It?

It is software used to improve how products and services are delivered to customers. In a small business this could be used to plan delivery routes in a more efficient manner, then in larger businesses this can scale up to managing complex delivery systems combining in-house delivery teams, as well as third-party logistics providers.

The scale and the tasks undertaken by the software will vary depending on the type of business, with a range of options available, including:

- Planning delivery routes to reduce fuel costs, reduce milage, and increase delivery efficiency.

- Driver information systems using mobile devices to advise on which route to take, which packages need to be dropped off or collected at each location, customer signatures or photo evidence of delivery and quality. This could also include GPS tracking of vehicles and stock for additional security.
- Workforce management to ensure shift patterns and employee absences are managed effectively to ensure the business can still deliver the products.
- Managing logistics companies to book collections and drop offs, as well as correctly labelling products.
- Providing updates to customers on the likely delivery times and gathering feedback.

Logistics is closely linked to warehouse, stock, and inventory management, and it's likely there will be some crossover between features of these software solutions, see 'Stock or Inventory Management' section to ensure all your requirements are captured.

How Do I Do It?

Due to the range of services available, and also the possible integrations with other systems, it's important to clearly understand your requirements. Creating a process map ('Process Map' section) of the business would be ideal, or as a minimum, just the dispatch area processes. Make sure to include the operations immediately before dispatch to completely capture what is required and to understand if any data needs to be shared from other systems. For example, if an order management system is in use to control production, it would make sense to automatically share some information with a logistics planning solution to avoid errors. Information such as order number, the delivery address, or expected delivery date maybe stored in the order management system and could automatically be sent to the logistics software on completion of the order.

Speak to the staff working in the dispatch area and the delivery drivers to understand their requirements, or what they find frustrating or time consuming in their work. This will help to find a solution which works for your business. Using user stories ('User Stories' section) is a good way of capturing this information, and then involve the staff in any demonstrations or discussions with potential suppliers to get their buy-in.

Finally, be clear about what data needs to be shared with other software applications and be explicit about these requirements when discussing with potential suppliers.

What Are the Benefits and Limitations?

✓ Reduction in paperwork, avoiding loss or damage of delivery notes, improving reliability.

✓ Reduction in fuel use, and more productive staff and fleet.

– It's likely that the software provider will be different from other providers used by the company, so ensure data sharing is easy and automated by discussing it with the supplier before placing the order.

Useful Search Terms

- Delivery/logistics planning software compatible with <<*current software system*>>.

- Route planning software for <<*product type/size, or vehicle type*>>.

MANUFACTURING RESOURCE PLANNING (MRP)

What Is It?

It is software used to manage all the elements required to produce products in a manufacturing company. Originally MRP stood for materials requirements planning, which solely concentrated on ensuring that the raw materials were delivered on time ready for production. This has evolved into manufacturing resource planning (MRP) which not only includes the materials, but also the staff, machinery, and anything else which is required to complete the production demands.

MRP systems will vary greatly depending on the industry that the company operates in, as well as things like the variation in products, the volume, range of manufacturing processes, and regulatory requirements. For example, compare the information and control required in a bakery making small batches of bread and cakes, to a company making components in the automotive industry, to a company processing logs. All will need to capture information on the raw materials, some will need detailed process information storing for each batch of product, but will differ in the skills of the staff, the equipment required, and the methods of manufacture. It's unlikely that each of those companies would be able to efficiently use the same MRP software, instead they should look for a solution which best fits their business, and they shouldn't significantly change how they operate to align with a software system.

How Do I Do It?

There are many MRP providers available, ranging from modules in large enterprise resource planning (ERP) systems ('Enterprise Resource Planning' section) designed for complex organisations, through to industry-specific providers, and systems designed for small producers with bespoke, high variation products.

Create a process map ('Process Map' section) of the main methods of manufacture for your key products, note where there are variations, such as fitting optional accessories or the addition of a required drying process. You may need to group products together with similar methods to simplify the process and make the task more manageable, make sure to note any differences so this can be accounted for in the MRP.

Decide on the data that is required at each step, where it will come from, any metrics to be used to monitor production, as well as any other systems that the data will need to be shared with to ensure the system runs efficiently. Capture this in a requirements document 'Requirements Capture – Software' section. Use these requirements to investigate and evaluate solution providers. It's important to assign someone to lead this project and allow them enough time to do it thoroughly.

For a manufacturing company an MRP system can cover a large amount of the business's processes, it's worth evaluating if an ERP system is more appropriate, because if an ERP system is implemented in the future there may be a significant amount of overlap it may not be cost effective, or it could be inefficient to run both. Use a software architecture map ('Software Architecture Diagram' section) to plan how they will work together and what data needs to be shared.

What Are the Benefits and Limitations?

✓ Improved understanding of production capacity, and other drivers affecting production performance.

✓ Many options are available, even for complex products or bespoke services.

✓ Clearer instructions to staff and improved understanding of day-to-day priorities.

– Software processes can be rigid and not flexible enough for a small business, discuss this with potential suppliers before implementation to ensure orders can be prioritised or adjusted if needed.

Useful Search Terms

- MRP software in <<*industry/manufacturing process type/product type*>>.
- MRP software for SME with <<*key requirement*>>. For example, "MRP software for SME with complex bill of materials".

ORDER TRACKING

What Is It?

It is a method of understanding the progress of each customer's orders through the production process. Using a method of gathering data at each stage of the process, staff or the customer will be able to see how the order has progressed and when it is expected to be finished. In businesses where office tasks are a significant proportion of the lead time, these tasks can be included in the tracking process, for example, bespoke design work, material ordering, prototype testing, or simulations of the design will be important and should be tracked.

Order tracking is related to shop floor data capture ('Shop Floor Data Capture' section) and manufacturing resource planning (MRP) ('Manufacturing Resource Planning' section) as the data needs to be collected from somewhere. Standalone systems can be installed which allow operators to mark jobs or operations as complete on a tablet or shop floor computer, while automated options using barcode or radio frequency identification (RFID) scanners can track products on production lines without manual intervention.

A key aspect is how the data is analysed and displayed. A dashboard, see 'Data Dashboards' and 'Business Intelligence Software' section, or customer portal ('Customer Portals' section) could be used to make the data accessible to those that need it, for example, the sales team could use it to update customers, or production leaders could use it to monitor progress on high priority orders.

How Do I Do It?

List the tasks which need to be completed from a customer placing an order through to it being dispatched or installed. Alternatively, a process map ('Process Map' section) of the business will also show the same information. Decide how often the system needs to be updated, if a product has to pass through a series of tasks which take 30 seconds each to complete, the operator shouldn't have to update the system manually after each one. Consider other important factors, such as key process bottlenecks, it might be worth increasing the amount of data collection before and after a crucial production process so that the flow of products can be monitored and optimised. Finally, decide how the data should be collected and displayed. Is the data available already and if so what format is it in, does the order tracking system need to integrate with other software solutions, does it need to be compatible with particular hardware like shop floor tablets, or is there business intelligence or data analysis software already in use that it will need to feed data into. Collate these in a requirements document ('Requirements Capture – Software' section).

Use these requirements to discuss solutions with technology providers, making sure to include the staff that will be using the system in the discussions and any software trials or demonstrations.

What Are the Benefits and Limitations?

✓ Clear understanding of order progress, with analysis providing data to feed into improvement projects targeting operations which take longer than planned or cause bottlenecks.

✓ Improved office productivity as customers can check where their orders are without calling the sales team.

– Data collection needs to be carefully considered, any manual data collection needs operators to understand why they need to do it in order for the system to work correctly.

Useful Search Terms

- Order tracking in <<*industry*>>.
- Production tracking system with <<*ERP/MRP/e-commerce software name*>> integration.

PRODUCTION PLANNING

What Is It?

It is software used to organise the daily and weekly activities needed to manufacture products according to the customer demand. This is a less complex version of a manufacturing resource planning (MRP) system ('Manufacturing Resource Planning' section) and is useful to improve the visibility of the production schedule. Using software to help with production planning is often a good first step for a company using paper processes, because there are low-cost options available, as well as more tailored solutions which will be more expensive.

Online project management or office productivity tools can be used to create a digital version of a T-card system or kanban process which would help to organise the daily production tasks, and are often free or low-cost for a small number of users. The benefit of this approach is that orders and manufacturing operations can be organised by important drivers, such as machine availability, order priority, or staff skills. Once this is done, because they are web-based, the production schedule can be viewed by those who need to see it and it can also be displayed on screens around the shop floor so everyone is clear what the priorities are. Automation and rules can also be added to improve the planning process, and data sharing with other systems, like customer relationship management ('Customer Relationship Management Software' section) or an online order form, can automatically create entries for new orders with all the required information already included.

For more complex businesses, dedicated production planning solutions are available, although they tend to include more aspects of the business and are sold as MRP systems, or as a module in enterprise resource planning (ERP) software ('Enterprise Resource Planning' section).

How Do I Do It?

Create a process map ('Process Map' section) of the order of manufacture for your key products, or for jobbing shops, list each of the manufacturing processes or cells in the factory which need to be included in the plan. This will help you to set up the system in a manner which most suits how your factory operates.

Many online tools have free trials and have templates for different uses, so it's worth trying a few out, and making a note of what works well for you and what doesn't, or what additional features you would like. Share the output of the plan regularly with the shop floor staff, and get their feedback on how it works and what could be improved. Systems like this work best when data is shared between other services, try creating rules so entries are created automatically when an order is received by email, or when an enquiry is made on a website.

Keep using the system, trying new features and learning what works well for you and the shop floor staff. As the business grows the use of the planning system can be expanded, and eventually you can migrate to an MRP or ERP solution, with the experience of these first trials helping you to scope the project more effectively.

What Are the Benefits and Limitations?

✓ A good introduction to digital planning tools, which can start off replicating a paper plan, adding automation and data sharing or data analysis step by step.

✓ Improved productivity and visibility of schedules throughout the business.

✓ Free trials are often available to try different approaches.

– Many options are available, make use of free trials and online tutorials to find the best fit.

Useful Search Terms

• Free online planning tools/free online project management tools.

• Automatically <<*perform task*>> from <<*software*>> to <<*planning software*>>.

QUALITY MANAGEMENT

What Is It?

It is software used to help understand and monitor defects in production, manage traceability, and improve compliance with any regulatory requirements. It can make the process of gaining certifications, such as ISO 9001,[3] more manageable by keeping important documents, procedures, and certifications up to date and accessible.

Understanding the quality of the parts being produced is important to help make improvements, reduce waste, improve productivity, and increase production capacity. In addition to this, in some industries the requirements for quality control are extensive. For example, a company making parts for the aerospace industry may need to keep extensive records for a number of years after a part has been made, including where the raw material came from, inspection information, what the method of manufacture was and how it was validated, which other parts were made in the same batch, to name a few. Similarly, a company in the food industry may have to hold recipe information, detailed allergen information for all ingredients, when the batches were made, and who they were sold to. Keeping track of all this information in a paper system will be time consuming, labour intensive, and will require a lot of storage space. A quality management system helps to digitise all this information and improve compliance with the processes by making it easier for the staff to comply with the requirements.

How Do I Do It?

An important starting point is to understand the regulatory requirements your company needs to comply with, and then the granular detail of what data is required to achieve these. Further to the examples mentioned above, tasks such as change control for product designs or methods of manufacture, document management, staff training records, or equipment calibration could be required in your industry, and making a comprehensive list of these requirements will help to find an appropriate software solution. Create a requirements document to describe this to suppliers ('Requirements Capture – Software' section).

Inputting and retrieving data into and out of the system should be as simple as possible. To achieve this, consider where the data is generated and specify the system to capture this information as early as possible. As an example, if you need to understand the reject rate or right first time measure for an inspection operation, look to make it easy for the operator to input the inspection results when they're taken, or look to automatically capture the data from the inspection equipment.

Quality management systems can be part of an enterprise resource planning (ERP) solution ('Enterprise Resource Planning' section), it may be that document management and change control is covered in the ERP system, but a separate software solution is needed for the dimensional inspection data in production. In this case, ensure that the data can be shared easily between the systems to avoid the possibility of losing data, incorrectly capturing data, or staff having to spend time manually copying data between systems. Use a software architecture diagram for this ('Software Architecture Diagram' section).

What Are the Benefits and Limitations?

✓ Target improvement projects by understanding quality data.

✓ Improve compliance with regulatory requirements.

✓ Reduce labour-intensive tasks relating to data management.

– The range of regulations across different industries means that it can be complex to set up, allow adequate time and resource to manage the project carefully.

– Elements of quality management could be split across different software solutions, clearly capture your requirements and detail what data needs to be shared.

Useful Search Terms

• Quality management software for <<*industry*>> or <<*ERP system*>>.

RESOURCE MANAGEMENT

What Is It?

It is software used to help plan the work assigned to members of staff, improving productivity, job satisfaction, and quality. This can be applied to any area of the business, both office based and on the shop floor. For a small team managing the workload of staff manually with paper systems or on whiteboards is common and can also be effective, but as teams expand within a growing business continuing with these processes can cause confusion, unbalanced teams, and reliance on one individual.

Similar to production planning, online project management or office productivity tools can be used to create a digital plan of who will be working on which task, customer order, or process. The benefit of having it online means that it's easily accessible by anyone who needs to see it, providing clarity and making operations more efficient. For example, a design team could assign tasks on a planning website, and the sales team could have visibility of the planning board, so that if they have a query from a customer or need to check on progress, they can go direct to the designer responsible for the particular task. Once it's set up rules and automations can be introduced, so that information is automatically shared between teams, for example, once the designer has finished their tasks, the software could send an alert to the purchasing team to say that the items are ready to be ordered, and the sales team can update the customer on the progress.

After using the system, the data it contains also allows analysis to identify where improvements can be made. For example, is there duplication in some tasks, is there often rework in others, or is there a shortage of a particular skill in the team.

How Do I Do It?

Many of the online planning or productivity tools offer free trials and are quick to set up, so it's easy to have a go and find out what works and what doesn't. Pick one area of the business to try the system, maybe where there are issues with lead times being longer than expected, where staff are overloaded, or where there are potential skills gaps. Talk to the staff in the team to explain what the plan is, and work with them to create a list of tasks, groups of skill sets, or a sequence of events that need to happen for every order. This will help with the initial set up of the system, and often there are templates or tutorials online providing detailed guidance on how to use the tools for specific purposes.

Ensure the team has visibility of the information and can openly feedback on how they think it works, and what can be improved. Learn from each trial and it's worth trying different options until you find one that works for your business. Going through this process will help you to define the requirements ('Requirements Capture – Software' section), as well as understand how the team works, make improvements, and in the future if you're looking at a resource management module in an enterprise resource planning (ERP) system it can help you decide what that needs to do.

What Are the Benefits and Limitations?

- ✓ Improved clarity of a team's workload and processes.
- ✓ Identify improvements and skill gaps which need to be filled.
- ✓ Low cost or free versions are available, which are easy to set up and try different options.
- – There are a lot of different approaches and tools available, but they're easy to quickly test.

Useful Search Terms

- • Free online planning tools/free online project management tools.
- • Automatically <<*perform task*>> from <<*software*>> to <<*planning software*>>.

SALES OR DEMAND FORECASTING

What Is It?

It is using software or data analysis techniques to predict the level of sales in the coming weeks, months, or years. Having accurate forecasts allows a company to improve production planning, implement targeted improvement projects, smooth peaks in production, and develop new products to fill spare capacity.

Advanced data analysis tools are now available online, either as standalone services or as part of larger software platforms, and forecasting tools based on statistical techniques are also included in most desktop spreadsheet software packages. With the development of more powerful computing systems, the use of artificial intelligence techniques such as machine learning and neural networks ('Artificial Intelligence' section) means that larger amounts of data can be analysed to bring out more subtle trends or correlations which would have otherwise been missed.

For example, taking a single data set from sales over the last five years could be analysed in a spreadsheet, producing a chart showing seasonal trends, and forecasted sales by month over the next year. More advanced analysis could be done in a sales or order management system, providing more granularity by product type or customer. Add in data sets from a manufacturing resource planning (MRP) system ('Manufacturing Resource Planning' section) as well as a stock control system ('Stock or Inventory Management' section), and you can create a more complex data model which might show links between how demand slows when lead times increase, or supplier lead times are longer at certain times of the year which affects delivery performance. Knowing these factors allows a more accurate forecast which enables targeted improvement activities.

How Do I Do It?

Predicting the future involves understanding risks and uncertainty, as well as understanding how reliable the data sets are. Many online services offer introductory training courses in data analysis, which would provide a good starting point to understand these aspects of forecasting.

Start by understanding the data that is already collected by the business, and perform some initial analysis on those data sets as an introduction. Identify where there are gaps in the data which are preventing you from making a more accurate forecast, and develop ways of collecting the additional information. Investigate if any of the software systems in use already offer forecasting modules, or if there are any available which can automatically extract data from your systems, as these will be easier to implement. Alternatively, investigate forecasting tools and ensure the data you collect can be exported and processed in the correct format, or if the data needs to be cleaned or organised first.

What Are the Benefits and Limitations?

✓ More efficient planning, improved stock management, and reduction in waste.

✓ More effective use of production capacity.

✓ Improved customer service.

– All predictions have assumptions and generalisations, it's important to understand the risks and uncertainties in the models and then making decisions taking everything into account.

Useful Search Terms

- Sales forecasting with <<*sales software*>>.
- Introduction to data analysis and forecasting training course.

SHOP FLOOR DATA CAPTURE

What Is It?

It is a method of gathering information from the production area in order to improve planning and optimise operations. There are a number of approaches to collecting data, such as:

- Paper charts filled in by the shop floor staff, which is a good way of quickly testing if the data is useful, although it can be time consuming and inaccurate.
- Tablets or computers on the shop floor to input data, which are used to collect information manually but in a form which is easier to analyse.
- Automated data collection from machines, either through the addition of sensors to collect data ('Industrial Internet of Things' section) or by using information gathered by the machine itself via the programmable logic controller (PLC).
- Manufacturing execution systems (MES) are software modules which include data capture as well as providing other services like displaying the correct drawings for the operation currently being performed, showing work instructions or standard operating procedures (SOP) ('Standard Operating Procedures' section). This could be a standalone software solution or part of a manufacturing requirements planning ('Manufacturing Requirements Planning' section) or enterprise resource planning (ERP) solution ('Enterprise Resource Planning' section).

Once the data is being collected it can be used to identify where improvements need to be made as well as reporting production status to other areas of the business, like sales or the leadership team, or directly to the customer.

How Do I Do It?

The first step is to understand the data that you need to collect by working backwards from what you want to achieve with the system. For example, if lead times are currently too long, then you'll need an accurate measure of the current cycle times of each operation and the amount of time a product is waiting in between. This could be gathered by using industrial internet of things (IIoT) sensors for machines and operators to use. It could also be gathered by operators scanning barcodes or selecting options on a rugged tablet, which are easier to implement, or a full MES system would also do this.

It's likely that there will be a number of reasons you want to gather data, which will require a variety of data collection methods. Make a list of these requirements and investigate solutions which can support them, as well as providing either suitable data analysis tools in the software or allowing you to extract the data automatically to another data analysis tool.

What Are the Benefits and Limitations?

- ✓ Basic systems are easy to implement and quickly gather useful data to make improvements.
- ✓ Improved understanding of how the business works and where changes are required to achieve the company's goals.
- ✓ MES provides up-to-date, version controlled information for each operation reducing the likelihood of defects.
- – Without operator buy-in the system could provide inaccurate data or none at all, engage the shop floor team early and explain the reasons and benefits of the project as well as how it will improve their jobs.

Useful Search Terms

- Shop floor data capture for <<*industry or production type*>>.
- Automatically collect data from <<*machine type or brand*>>.

STOCK OR INVENTORY MANAGEMENT

What Is It?

It is software used to keep track of all items like raw material, component parts, or finished products the company has in storerooms and warehouses. This can have a number of benefits including reducing time spent on stock taking, improving the feed in process to the manufacturing area, improving the dispatch operations, and making purchasing tasks more efficient.

Manufacturing companies use and manage stock in different ways depending on the industry and the types of products and processes involved. As with other software systems there are a large number of options to choose from, some are industry specific, and some are more general which require setting up or modifying to suit each business. For example, a company assembling electronic circuit boards and wiring looms would use high numbers of discrete components, some of which will be high value yet very small, and the stock system would need to account for these accurately. It's likely this would be installed with a barcode system to mark locations on the shelves or in the storage units so that it's easier to manage. Compare that to a company manufacturing bespoke steel structures, which would buy in stock sizes of steel sheet or bar, and then use the material as it's required for an order, returning the remainder to the stores. This system would need to be able to account for partial quantities of material, rather than discrete numbers of items.

How Do I Do It?

Understand what you want the system to do by looking at elements such as the number of product types, how material is consumed (in individual units or by length or weight), which other software systems it will need to share data with, how the storage area is currently laid out, how your staff would prefer to input data (using computers, tablets, or barcode scanners), and where they will need to input this data.

Next, consider the information you would like to get out of the system to help with managing stock and reporting important information to other areas of the business. This may include features like automatic reordering from suppliers based on low stock levels of critical components, alerts when stock levels reach a certain point, or allocating particular materials to specific orders either manually or by linking with other software systems.

Once the software requirements are understood it's easier to find a software solution which fits your company the best, rather than trying to change how your company operates to fit some software. Investigate software solutions which are made for your industry or type of product as these may be quicker to set up and more suited to your operations, but bear in mind that many generic stock management systems can be easily customised and might be a better fit. Finally, some elements of warehouse automation ('Warehouse Automation' section) may be suitable, which is worth considering at this stage.

What Are the Benefits and Limitations?

✓ Accurate understanding of stock levels without having to physically check or count items.

✓ Faster storeroom operations, reducing time to find stock, and avoiding manual errors.

✓ Improved understanding of material use and more cost-effective raw material purchasing.

– Staff may need to perform additional data entry tasks, ensure they understand the benefits of the system and are included from the start so they have a say which will work best for them.

Useful Search Terms

- Stock/inventory management for <<*industry/material type/manufacturing type*>>.
- Barcode and stock management systems to integrate with <<*other software system in use*>>.

BLOCKCHAIN

What Is It?

It is a method of securing records, as blocks, by creating many copies on different computers across different networks. The system can then spot if one record has been tampered with because it doesn't match all the other copies on the other computers. This makes the information more secure than having it stored on a single central database. It also means that different people or companies can have access to only the information that they need to see. The technology is used in cryptocurrencies, but also offers potential uses in manufacturing industries, such as:

- Logistics or complex stock control where data integrity is critical, or where many people need quick access to specific bits of information.
- Supply chain management for the traceability of materials or products from different suppliers.

How Do I Do It?

The technology is suited to larger companies or companies which are involved in large or complex supply chains. And while it has been used in cryptocurrencies for a number of years, it is also relatively early days for applications in manufacturing, logistics, and supply chains.

Setting up a blockchain system from scratch will require agreement from all the companies involved in the supply chain, for example, which data will be accessible by who, how it will be managed, when it will be updated, which other parties can the data be shared with, and what the validation criteria are for adding new members to the system. Once this is established, a specialist developer with skills in blockchain systems will be required to scope the project in detail, including which other software systems it will need to interface with at each company, and then start to build and test it.

Alternatively, your company may be invited to join a system established by a larger company or network of suppliers. In this case it's important to fully understand how your data will be used and which other companies or people will have access to your data. Similarly, take the time to learn about the system and find out if there is any information within it which would make your operations more effective, as this will benefit the entire supply chain.

What Are the Benefits and Limitations?

- ✓ Share data between companies, sites, or departments in a controlled manner, regardless of the software in use at each one.
- ✓ Accurate traceability for materials or products across complex supply chains.
- – The technology is in its infancy in the manufacturing sector, especially for SMEs.
- – Specialist skills and a detailed understanding of the system are crucial to ensure data security.

Useful Search Terms

- Blockchain solutions for <<*industry type or logistics/supply chain challenge*>>.

3D SCANNING

What Is It?

It is using a non-contact device to collect information about the size and shape of items. Once the data is collected software can be used to take accurate measurements from the 3D model or it can be imported into a computer-aided design (CAD) package to be modified and developed. Some common uses for 3D scanning equipment are:

- Dimensional inspection, comparing a part or component to the technical drawing or CAD model to decide if it is within tolerance or not.
- Reverse engineering components, quickly creating a 3D CAD model of an old or obsolete part which doesn't have a detailed drawing or model which can be used to make a replacement.
- Design development, measuring spaces, or other parts that a new component needs to fit into or interface with. For example, measuring the empty spaces under the bonnet of a car to retrofit components to, or scanning a handmade prototype to create mould tools for volume production.
- Measuring the interior and exterior of buildings to allow detailed planning of equipment installation or building modifications.

There are two main technologies used in 3D scanning – camera-based and laser systems. Camera-based systems include photogrammetry which uses a series of 2D photographs to build up a 3D model of a subject, and 3D structured light systems which project a pattern onto the subject and use offset cameras to determine the depth from the 2D images, which are also then built up into a 3D model. Laser systems use individual laser points to gather the coordinates of points on the surface of the subject. Laser line systems use a series of laser points in a row and scan across the surface of the subject to collect hundreds or thousands of data points at a time. There is a significant overlap in the capabilities of the camera-based and laser systems, both have their strengths and weaknesses, so either can be considered for many tasks.

There are also options for how the scanner is held and manipulated to gather the data. Low-cost handheld scanners are available which can quickly gather size and shape information at an adequate resolution for many tasks. For more accurate measurements the scanner could be mounted onto a robot arm or a CNC machine head, and adding a measurement fixture with reference points to a known datum will further increase the accuracy of the system.

How Do I Do It?

The first consideration is how accurate the data needs to be. It would be acceptable for the scan of the inside of a building to be accurate to the nearest 5 to 10 mm, whereas the scan of an engine component for a Formula 1 car may need to be accurate to 5 microns. The accuracy of the system is also dependent on a number of other factors, such as the surface finish, the material properties, how shiny or reflective the surface is, the temperature stability of the room, and the ambient light conditions. If these are an issue they can be addressed through controlled lighting, coating the subject in powder, or adding sticker dots to provide regular reference points.

Any scanner will output a series of points, called a point cloud, and software will be required to convert this into a solid CAD model which can then be imported into a CAD package. The provider of the scanner will be able to advise on appropriate post-processing software to achieve this.

What Are the Benefits and Limitations?

- ✓ Quickly gather data on complex geometries for a range of applications.
- ✓ Replaces manual measurements providing a full 3D model of an object or space.
- ✓ Scanning can be performed as a service or equipment can be hired as a way of testing different options.
- – The measurement accuracy can be affected by a number of factors, if this is important ensure detailed accuracy checks are performed in different conditions and on representative features before selecting a solution, and the system is calibrated regularly during operation.

Useful Search Terms

- 3D scanner to measure <<*product type*>> or to <<*accuracy required*>>.
- Non-contact measurement providers in <<*location*>>.

4G AND 5G NETWORKS OR PRIVATE NETWORKS

What Is It?

It is a method of networking devices over a large site, as an alternative to Wi-Fi. 4G and 5G refer to the fourth and fifth generations of mobile communication technology, which is normally associated with mobile phones, but it can also be set up as a network within a company's site. The technology has a number of advantages over Wi-Fi, mainly:

- Longer range, which means fewer transmitters/network points/signal boosters are needed.
- Faster and more reliable switching between network points, which gives moving devices a more reliable connection.
- More devices can be connected to the network, and important devices can be given priority so they never lose connection.

Setting up a private network using 4G or 5G would be suitable for a site with either large buildings or a number of buildings where getting Wi-Fi signal is difficult, or where data connection is critical to a machine or area operating properly. For example:

- Robotic cells or critical machines which are controlled remotely by software or a computer from a different area of the site. These could be fitted with a 5G device and connected to a private network, so that the controller has a guaranteed connection and can respond to changes immediately, without risking errors in production.
- A large warehouse where operators use mobile phones, tablets, and autonomous mobile robots (AMRs) to locate and retrieve stock, but Wi-Fi is unreliable or there is a lot of interference on the Wi-Fi signal. Each device could connect to the 5G network as the range is better, and they can be confident that the signal is reliable.

How Do I Do It?

The 5G network uses similar frequencies to mobile networks, and these are regulated by national governments. In the UK a band of frequencies has been allocated for local 5G networks,[4] and a particular frequency can be reserved in a local area for a small fee, by a company or an individual. The first step is to investigate the availability and cost of reserving a frequency where your company operates.

Plan the area you need the network to cover and create a comprehensive list of the types of devices which will need to be connected. Machines or equipment may not be compatible with 5G in their current state, and these will need an adapter installing or retrofitting. Discuss these requirements with network providers to understand the costs, installation methods, number of antennae needed, timescales, training, connections to other software or internal networks, and the suitability of your site.

What Are the Benefits and Limitations?

- ✓ Faster and more reliable connection for machinery and handheld devices.
- ✓ Longer range than Wi-Fi.
- ✓ More flexible connection options, allowing key equipment to have priority.
- – The initial costs of the equipment and antennae can be high, so consider the business case for improved productivity in areas with poor connection and the opportunities for connected machines.
- – It won't necessarily improve internet connection speeds as the network is separate from the internet service provider.

Useful Search Terms

- Private 5G network providers in <<location>>.
- Frequency band or spectrum allocation in <<country>>.

COMPUTER-AIDED DESIGN (CAD) INCLUDING SIMULATION AND DESIGN AUTOMATION

What Is It?

It is software used to create and edit designs in 2D or 3D. CAD is now widespread in many industries. Initially it was just used to replace manual drawing on paper and drawing boards, and as technology has improved the uses now include 3D modelling, photorealistic visualisation, simulation of product performance, customer modification, manufacturing planning, and creation of shop floor instructions to name just a few. Computer-aided manufacture (CAM) is now generally included in the CAD software, but originally it was used to write the production files needed for a machine to create a part.

Many industries have standard software packages which are used, for example, the construction industry will use a different package to aerospace manufacturing, but CAD models can be exchanged using common file formats such as .step or .stl. Once a model is created in CAD it can be evaluated in different modules, such as creating manufacturing stage drawings, performing cost calculations, checking material properties, and some allow models to be modified by different people simultaneously to speed up product development. Simulation is now extremely advanced and reliable allowing users to check how a product will perform under certain conditions. Or, how successful a production process will be, like injection moulding or casting, and then iterate the design to reduce waste material, improve cycle time, or optimise surface finish in a machining process.

How Do I Do It?

Identify what you intend to use the software for, such as sharing models with customers or suppliers, any potential future uses for the software, and if people in the business have training or extensive experience with a particular software package. These are important because there is a large amount of learning involved with using a new CAD package, and while it is often beneficial and will have a positive impact on the business, selecting something which isn't compatible with the programs suppliers use, for example, will make processes very inefficient.

After selecting a software package, identify key users for the different elements, and allow appropriate time for them to complete training and to familiarise themselves with how the different features work. It's good practice to write guidelines or house rules for how to perform different tasks, as there are often a number of different ways to achieve the same result, such as drawing a 2D profile, and ensuring everyone in the team approaches it in the same way makes it easier to share work and make improvements.

Building on this, creating design rules can be useful for companies where designs are often bespoke but follow a set of principles, many software packages allow users to create design automations, where the designer inputs key parameters and the 3D model is automatically created. This can also be linked to a website, where the same logic is used, and customers can input their requirements, and instantly receive a rendered model of what it would look like, and a quote based on up-to-date material and production costs.

Alternatively, if the use of a CAD package is a small element of the company's activities, then it can be outsourced to freelance CAD designers or CAD consultants.

What Are the Benefits and Limitations?

✓ Fast iteration of designs through simulation or improved data sharing with stakeholders.

✓ Allow customers to create their own designs and quotes to certain design rules.

✓ Easily manage design history and store all project data digitally with a product data management (PDM) system.

− Sharing files between CAD packages can lose key information due to the different file formats, check models carefully after converting them to make sure the information needed is still accurate.

Useful Search Terms

• CAD in <<*industry*>> or <<*product or process used*>>.

• Simulation software for <<*product or process type*>>.

• CAD package with e-commerce integration or design automation.

CLOUD COMPUTING

What Is It?

It is processing and storing data using offsite servers or computers which are managed by another company. This means that the computing power required to perform tasks is not in your building, but probably in a large data centre, so you don't have to invest in powerful computers and the data can be accessed from anywhere with an internet connection.

Traditionally a factory would have a server or a computer which ran their software and stored all the data on site, with backups of the data taken periodically and stored offsite in case of a fire or another emergency. This would require the company to invest in the equipment, set it up, and maintain it correctly to ensure that it runs effectively avoiding any disruption to the business. As internet speeds and the computing power in data centres have increased, it's now often more efficient for a company to offer the data processing and storage as a service, usually with a monthly or annual subscription fee, allowing the factory to operate without having to manage the server on their own.

Many of the software modules described on the other sections of this book will be available through a cloud computing platform. For example, a cloud-based enterprise resource planning (ERP) system ('Enterprise Resource Planning' section) would store all the company's data offsite in the data centre, and the staff in the factory would access the data through a computer, phone, or tablet using an app or an internet browser. This means they could process orders, contact customers, check stock levels, and generate reports easily, but all the information is stored offsite, is accessible from anywhere, and the company doesn't need to invest as much in hardware. Even tasks which require large amounts of processing power, such as computer-aided design (CAD) or complex simulations ('Computer-aided Design' section), can now be run through cloud services, which could represent a significant saving in hardware costs.

How Do I Do It?

Cloud computing isn't something that is done in isolation, it's a service provided as part of a system or software platform. Look at the tasks that need to be performed in your factory, and identify an appropriate solution, such as manufacturing resource planning (MRP) ('Manufacturing Resource Planning' section), CAD, simulation, customer relationship management ('Customer Relationship Management' section), or data storage, and as part of your research look for companies which offer this as a cloud service. The security of your data is an important consideration when looking to use cloud computing, so ensure you look into this carefully and are satisfied that it will be protected and that you'll be compliant with regulations such as general data protection regulations (GDPR). Cloud computing can also make sharing data with other systems easier, so check for integrations with other software services or if application programming interfaces (APIs) are available.

What Are the Benefits and Limitations?

✓ All data is stored and processed offsite, reducing the amount of investment required and increasing the security, while improving access for people who need it.

✓ Cloud software versions are often updated regularly, with new features added.

✓ People with the appropriate approvals can access the data from wherever they need to.

− Access will be limited by the speed of the internet connection, so check the minimum speed required for each service.

Useful Search Terms

- <<*Software type or task*>> cloud solution/provider.
- Cloud data storage solutions.
- API integration for <<*software 1*>> to <<*software 2*>>.

INDUSTRIAL INTERNET OF THINGS (IIOT)

What Is It?

The internet of things (IoT) is a term used to describe the addition of connectivity to everyday items in order to make them more useful or convenient. Examples would be smart thermostats or smart light bulbs, items which wouldn't normally be connected to the internet but now can be as the technology has become cheaper. The result is a user can control their heating from their phone, or set the lights to come on automatically at sunset, powered by IoT.

The industrial internet of things (IIoT) applies this thinking to industrial settings, such as machines, buildings, or even people through the use of sensors. In manufacturing this could be used to:

- Understand which machines are used more often and which have spare capacity, see overall equipment effectiveness ('Overall Equipment Effectiveness' section).
- Measure energy use on individual pieces of equipment ('Energy Monitoring' section).
- Monitor process variables to improve quality ('Key Process Variable Control' section).
- Measure air quality or meeting room use.
- Track the location of key pieces of equipment.
- Monitor machine health and alert when maintenance is needed.

How Do I Do It?

Some modern machines will have IoT functions built in already, although a subscription fee maybe required to use the software provided by the manufacturer. Check the manufacturer's website or machine specification and look for Industry 4.0 or connectivity features.

Alternatively, low-cost sensors are available and can be easily fitted to existing equipment. For example, a current clamp can be fitted around the power cable of a machine and this will measure the amount of power used, when the machine is used, if it is left in idle during breaks, and the electricity cost during this time. The sensors will need a gateway device which collects the information from the sensors and sends it to a software platform on the internet where it can be viewed and analysed. Gateways look like a broadband router, and can be wired or wireless, and in some cases they can analyse the information without needing an internet connection, this is called edge computing. Many different sensor types can connect to a single gateway, meaning one gateway could gather the power use data from a number of machines, the temperature in the office, how often different meeting rooms are used, as well as if a door to a controlled room has been left open.

What Are the Benefits and Limitations?

- ✓ Easy to quickly gather data.
- ✓ Entry-level sensors are low cost.
- ✓ Large range of sensors and services.
- ✓ Subscription models are accessible.
- ✓ Excellent starting point for net zero.
- – Bespoke services can be expensive, use a requirements document ('Requirements Capture – Hardware' section) and business case ('Building a Business Case' section) to make sure it provides value for money.
- – The number of technology terms can be confusing, speak to the technology provider to understand the benefits of each, or research them online.

Useful Search Terms

- • Machine monitoring in <<*industry*>>.
- • Remote machine monitoring in manufacturing.
- • Real-time production monitoring.
- • Building management system.
- • IIoT providers in <<*industry*>> or <<*location*>>.

BUILDING INFORMATION MODELLING (BIM)

What Is It?

It is a method of providing digital models and additional information about products and processes used in the construction industry. This information is stored in a BIM file, CAD file, or in BIM marketplaces, and is useful to people involved in the design, construction, and maintenance of new buildings. A new building requires the involvement of a large number of people, from architects, civil engineers, planning departments, utilities providers, through to maintenance teams and the end user of the building, to name a few. BIM aims to improve the communication and information sharing between each of these people by using digital technology.

As a manufacturer supplying to the construction industry BIM could:

- Raise awareness of your products, by listing them in BIM marketplaces allowing designers to easily select the most appropriate product for their needs.
- Improve development lead times for bespoke products, by better understanding requirements and sharing information with customers.
- Improve product performance by providing accurate installation and maintenance instructions.

How Do I Do It?

BIM is a broad term covering a large number of processes and products, and how to approach it depends on your position in the industry. Start by researching the technology online, discussing with BIM specialists, or your customers and suppliers, to understand what's appropriate for you.

For a manufacturer of products used in the construction industry such as heating systems, building lighting, building materials, or street furniture, there are a number of BIM marketplaces where models can be uploaded for architects and engineers to access when designing a building. The model will include meta data, or additional information, which will help the user select the right product, such as energy consumption, installation requirements, minimum or maximum air flow requirements, or data sheets.

What Are the Benefits and Limitations?

✓ Increased awareness of products in the marketplace.

✓ Larger building companies are mandating the use of BIM, adopting it will allow access to these markets.

✓ Reduced development lead times for bespoke products or systems.

– There can be costs associated with hosting products on BIM marketplaces.

Useful Search Terms

- BIM consultant/specialist in <<*location*>>.
- BIM marketplace for <<*product type*>>.

ENERGY MONITORING

What Is It?

It is the process of measuring and analysing how much energy is used in the factory, in order to reduce costs and improve efficiency. Energy costs are often a significant proportion of a manufacturing business's outgoings, so understanding which areas or machines consume the most allows a targeted approach to reduce the costs, and understand the scope 1 or scope 2 emissions, as part of a carbon reduction plan. A range of options are available:

- Smart meters are normally supplied by the electricity provider and are used to gather the electricity or gas used for the entire site, at an interval of 30 minutes. This will help to understand the broad trends in energy use, such as how much is used during downtime, peak production, or at evenings and weekends. If usage is still high when the factory isn't in use, then it may be that heating or cooling systems are still active, compressors are still running, or machines are still using power in idle mode.
- For a more granular understanding of energy use by area, individual monitors can be installed on the building's power supply. This would allow an analysis of energy use in the machining area compared to the offices and warehouse, for example.
- The energy usage of individual machines can be measured using current monitors installed in the control cabinet. These can be very low cost and take a matter of minutes to install, using a gateway to send the data to an online service for analysis. Some services provide additional information which is inferred from the energy data to improve production planning, such as cycle time measures, productivity analysis, and maintenance alerts. See 'Industrial Internet of Things' section.

How Do I Do It?

The best place to start for a general overview of the site's energy use is to install a smart meter. This will help understand the costs as well as identify where some quick improvements can be made. It's likely that more granular data will be required, using either monitors on the building power supply or individual sensors on machines. To do this, identify which areas or machines are likely to have a higher usage, and decide whether it's more appropriate to measure machines individually with IIoT sensors or if the general area will be sufficient.

Once the data is being collected it is crucial to analyse it regularly and take action to address any issues that are identified. The energy monitoring on its own won't reduce the power use, but checking use by shift, by week, or by month and then putting measures in place to use less power will make a difference.

What Are the Benefits and Limitations?

✓ Understand energy use and identify where improvements can be made to reduce costs.

✓ A great starting point for net zero plans, helping to understand scope 1 and scope 2 emissions ('Net Zero' section).

✓ Initial energy monitoring options are low cost and can identify significant savings.

– Support maybe required in analysing the data, look for online courses or local business support agencies.

Useful Search Terms

• Industrial smart meter installation for <<*energy provider or location*>>.

• Manufacturing machine energy monitoring.

• Energy monitoring consultants in <<*location*>>.

KEY PROCESS VARIABLE (KPV) CONTROL

What Is It?

It means understanding the factors which directly affect the quality and performance of a production process, then putting methods in place to control them. There will often be many variables which can be adjusted on any manufacturing process, but it's likely that there will be a few which are most important, and these are the key process variables KPVs, the ones which should be monitored and controlled to within a defined tolerance.

For example, in a bakery during the mixing process, a recipe calls for 300g of flour and from experience the baker knows that getting the wrong amount of flour affects the quality of the bread. This is one process variable, but before controls can be put in place it's necessary to understand the control limits – in this case, is the quality of the bread still acceptable if there's 301g or flour, or 310g? Once these limits are understood, the baker can put a tolerance range on the weight of flour, which might be between 295g and 310g. To control this, the work instruction could be updated to inform the operator how much it is acceptable to add, or for a tighter control the weighing process could be automated so that mistakes are less likely.

Each process will have different variables and they will affect the quality of the product by different amounts. In the bakery, the baking process is one of the most important, and the KPVs could include the temperature of the oven, how long the bread is in the oven for, and how many loaves are in at once, so these should have tighter controls in place.

How Do I Do It?

The first step is to decide on which are the critical operations in your process, or where you have the most quality issues, and address them one by one. Speaking to the people involved with the process will give a good indication of what the variables are. A welder would be able to explain what gives them a good join – the amount of current applied, the speed the weld torch is moved at, the quality of the weld preparation, or geometry of the material, for example.

To gain a more in-depth understanding of the process, a statistical process called 'design of experiments' ('Design of Experiments (DoE) and Statistical Analysis' section) will identify the KPVs and give an indication of how much impact they have on the output.

Once the KPVs are defined, investigate methods of controlling them, with instructions to operators being the most straightforward but can be the least effective, through to fully automating the control system, which should be the most effective.

What Are the Benefits and Limitations?

- ✓ Improved quality and process understanding.
- ✓ Understanding the KPVs allows more effective scoping of equipment and work instructions, as well as improved outsourcing of operations.
- – Installing new control systems can be time consuming and costly, perform trials first to ensure that the correct variables are being

controlled and use thorough requirements documents when working with suppliers ('Requirements Capture – Hardware section to 'Requirements Capture – Software' section).

Useful Search Terms

- Control systems for <<*manufacturing process*>>.
- Common key process variables for <<*manufacturing process*>>.

RADIO FREQUENCY IDENTIFICATION (RFID) AND BARCODING

What Is It?

It is the process of using labels with barcodes or embedded computer chips to improve operations and product tracking. RFID chips are common in non-contact bank cards, transport tickets, or store security systems. When placed near a tag reader, the reader sends a signal which provides enough power to the cards' chip for it to respond with some pre-programmed information. Alternatively, barcodes can be used in a similar way to provide a small amount of data to a reader, but without the need for a computer chip in the label. The original vertical stripes barcodes are useful for a short code, such as a product ID, whereas QR (quick read) codes are made up of a series of squares and can hold much more information. The RFID labels can cost as little as a few pence each, and so it's feasible to apply them to a large number of products or items in a business to gather more accurate data.

Some example uses in a manufacturing business are:

- Tracking products as they progress through the production line. Place a reader at certain checkpoints, and each time a tag is detected it sends an update to a piece of software, such as production planning ('Production Planning' section) or warehouse management software ('Warehouse Automation' section) to say where the item is.
- Quickly allow operators to check into and out of jobs or access relevant information. RFID or barcodes could be placed next to an operator's workspace so they could use their phone to scan the tag or barcode. This could either send a message to software saying they've started or finished an operation, or it could provide a link to the correct work instruction or a video demonstrating how to perform a task.

- Quick and accurate stock tracking. Having an RFID tag on each product in a warehouse would allow very quick stock takes as each item would have a unique number encoded into it, which the reader would recognise and send to the stock system, allowing it to be accounted for. Using barcodes for this would mean an operator manually scanning each product.
- Active RFID tags include a battery and can perform more advanced tasks, such as detecting movement or measuring temperature and humidity, to inform if a product has been treated correctly during storage or in transit.

How Do I Do It?

RFID tags on their own are unlikely to provide a benefit; this comes from how the data is used. Because of this and due to the range of applications of RFID and barcodes, there are a large number of providers and products available. The first step is to clearly understand your requirements, by having an idea of what you want the tags and the wider system to do for you ('Requirements Capture – Hardware' section to 'Requirements Capture – Software' section). At this point start to gather information such as the number of tags the system will have to cope with, what will happen with the data once it's been scanned, and which other software services it will need to be connected to. Research suppliers which are capable of providing a solution to suit your needs and discuss your requirements with them. It's recommended to test the range and speed at which the system can read the information, as well as check the interfaces with your existing software, to make sure it's suitable.

What Are the Benefits and Limitations?

- ✓ Tags and labels are low cost and can quickly provide useful information.
- ✓ Reduce time taken for tracking jobs or performing stock takes.
- – The tags or barcodes will need to be integrated with another system to make use of the data.

Useful Search Terms

- RFID provider in <<*industry*>> or <<*location*>>.
- RFID for <<*manufacturing process task*>> or <<*industry*>>.

SUPERVISORY CONTROL AND DATA ACQUISITION (SCADA)

What Is It?

It is a control system which sits over the machines and other equipment on the shop floor to provide a complete overview of the production process. The control system provides a visual representation of the production line, along with key information such as speeds, levels, pressures, and temperatures. This allows operators to oversee the entire process and make sure it is operating correctly, and in some cases the operator can make adjustments to bring a process back into tolerance, or these can be controlled automatically by the software.

For example, in a chemical processing line which has a number of vats of different liquids that need to be mixed to a set recipe, using SCADA the operator could check the levels in each vat, the flow rate of the liquids through the pipes, and monitor the temperatures. The system would display an alert to show the ratio is outside of the set range, and the operator would then make changes to one or more of these on the software, which would instruct the valves to automatically adjust the flow rates to ensure the correct ratios are achieved.

How Do I Do It?

Implementing a SCADA system requires the definition of each key process variable (KPV) for each stage of the production process, as well as an idea of the tolerance ranges for them ('Key Process Variable (KPV) Control' section). This is because the software needs to be told what is being monitored and when to alert that something is wrong.

Create a process map ('Process Map' section) of the entire production process, noting the KPVs for each one, and how they are currently measured and controlled. The SCADA system will rely on automatic measurement systems, and a digital measurement system will need to be installed for anything that is currently measured manually. At this point agree on the boundary of the system – where the control will start and stop, which operations or processes are to be included, and which will be left out.

The details of the machines and their control systems will also be important to the system integrator, as the SCADA software will need to connect to the programmable logic controller (PLC) in order to gather information such as the machine state, speeds, levels, and other critical status data.

Research SCADA system integrators which have the experience of dealing with similar equipment and processes to your factory. Use the process map, KPV information, and the PLC specifications to start to scope out your requirements with them ('Requirements Capture – Hardware' section to 'Requirements Capture – Software' section).

What Are the Benefits and Limitations?

- ✓ Improved product quality, machine availability, and higher operator productivity.
- ✓ Allows preventative maintenance and longer machine life.
- ✓ In hazardous processes SCADA allows remote monitoring and control, improving health and safety of the workforce.
- – Detailed understanding of the KPVs is required for each stage of the process, ensure these are clearly stated to the supplier as well as tolerance ranges for each.

Useful Search Terms

- SCADA in <<*industry*>>.
- SCADA system for <<*machine type or manufacturing process*>>.
- SCADA integrator in <<*location*>>.

WASTE MANAGEMENT

What Is It?

It is controlling and reducing the amount of waste generated by the business, and where waste is unavoidable, ensuring that it is disposed of responsibly through reusing or recycling. In a manufacturing business, the creation of waste material is often a necessity in order to produce the products – cutting a complex profile from a sheet of steel will inevitably leave offcuts, some of which are too small to be used elsewhere in production, or during the casting process, the runners and risers are required to feed the molten material into the mould, but are not a useful part of the end product. Actively managing the waste will help to reduce the amount of this material which can't be used, reducing material purchase costs, reducing disposal costs, and improving the company's scope 3 emissions (see 'Net Zero' section).

How Do I Do It?

There is a common hierarchy of waste: prevent, reduce, reuse, recycle, recover, and dispose. This encourages an approach of looking at the full lifecycle, primarily avoiding using material in the first place, using less when it is necessary, reusing any material where possible, recycling the waste material, recovering the energy from the material, and finally disposing of it as a last resort.

Waste management starts with the design of the product, in particular the material selection. Review the materials used, and check for alternatives which can improve the waste management process, such as those sourced from recycled materials, or reducing the amount of waste through improved quality, or standardise materials to reduce the number of waste streams created. Also consider if near net-shape is suitable, for example, rather than machining from a solid block could the component be cast or forged first, to reduce the amount of machining, although be careful that the waste isn't pushed into another part of your supply chain.

Review where waste is created and measure the amount, engage all your staff in this process, to help build up a picture of where to focus your efforts. At this point you can create separate waste streams, so that material is split into different types to improve how it is processed. If scrap material can be fed back into the production process, make this as easy as possible, and if it can't, make sure the recycling collection points are clear and easy to access. The companies you use for disposing of the waste should also be able to provide you with information about how much of each type of waste they collect from you, and what they do with it. This will help to decide on where to focus the improvement effort.

Finally, an increasing number of companies are being set up with the purpose of processing waste and making it reusable, such as grinding plastic components to create filament for 3D printing or insulation materials. It's worth researching companies that could process your waste in this way to support the circular economy.

What Are the Benefits and Limitations?

- ✓ Reduced costs of raw material and potentially reduced costs for disposal of waste.
- ✓ Improved understanding of the waste streams and scope 3 emissions contributions.

- Changing material types for products could require additional validation, depending on the industry, so take this into account when planning the change.
- More sustainable waste processing sources maybe more costly, but this could be balanced by the waste reduction efforts elsewhere in your process.

Useful Search Terms

- Waste processing/recycling/reprocessing company for <<*material type*>>.
- Sustainable alternatives to <<*material type*>>.

AUGMENTED REALITY, MIXED REALITY, AND EXTENDED REALITY

What Is It?

Augmented reality (AR) overlays information on to the user's view of the world, normally through a phone or a special headset. Mixed reality (MR) is similar to AR, and while there isn't a set definition, it allows the user to interact with the data, and extended reality (XR) is an overarching term covering everything to do with AR and MR. The three terms are often used interchangeably, so it's not critical to pick the right one. A manufacturing company could use XR in the following ways:

- Improve the customer experience by allowing them to use their phone to see how a product would look in their room. Using an app and the phone's camera, the user would see a 3D model of the product, such as a lamp or some furniture, overlayed onto the camera's image of their room. They could then select different colours or styles until they find the best fit.
- Create interactive instructions, using either a phone or an AR headset to improve quality. In production an operator or maintenance engineer could wear a headset, and see instructional videos relevant to the task they're performing, side by side with the real-life product, or they could see checklists or 3D models showing the step-by-step instructions. Similarly, a customer could use their phone or tablet to

work through assembly or operating instructions for the product, to ensure it is installed or built correctly.

- Provide remote support from specialists in a different location. Again, using a tablet or headset, the user could share what they see via a video call with a specialist engineer or consultant, to help with problem-solving. For example, when looking at the inside of an electrical cabinet, the specialist could annotate the view showing the correct connection to check, and the wearer would be able to see these notes overlaid in their field of view, so that they could be confident in what they're doing.

- Remotely collaborate on product development. Using headsets, the design team members could meet with the manufacturing team members to all view the same 3D model in space in front of them. They could discuss the design features and how they will be made in production, while modifying the design in real time to resolve any issues.

How Do I Do It?

There is a large range of devices and software systems which support XR. As such it's important to clearly capture your requirements ('Requirements Capture – Hardware' section to 'Requirements Capture – Software' section). Think about what you need the system to do, what type of CAD models and systems you use at the moment, which type of device would be more appropriate for your use case, and if it will use live data, what format will it be in, and which system would it come from. Look into suppliers which can provide this service and ask for demonstrations of similar work they have completed, to give you confidence that it will work for your company.

What Are the Benefits and Limitations?

- ✓ The creation of AR mobile apps for use by customers is accessible to small companies and can set them apart from competitors.
- ✓ Reduce travel time and costs by providing high-quality remote support from specialists.
- ✓ Improve training by creating engaging content which provides relevant information when the user needs it.

- Headsets are often restricted to what software can be used with them, so make sure your requirements are clear when discussing with suppliers.
- With the exception of remote support which can be supplied as an off-the-shelf service, other use cases for XR will be bespoke or require customisation by a specialist provider.

Useful Search Terms

- AR developer in <<*location*>>.
- AR integration with <<*CAD software or other data source*>>.
- AR software/systems for SME manufacturers.

DIGITAL TWIN

What Is It?

It is a virtual copy of a real-world object combined with a data feed from the object showing its current status. This can be manipulated, analysed, assessed, simulated, or inspected to help with the real-world object's operation. For example, a digital twin of a factory could start off as a CAD model of the building and the machines within it, information could be added to this such as maintenance information, location of control valves, and live data showing the number of people in each room, temperatures, or the position of parts on the shop floor. The digital twin would be useful for the maintenance team to refer to in order to find out where machine isolation points are and their status, while viewing service instructions. At the same time, the management team could see how meeting rooms are used, to adjust room booking or heating systems to make them more efficient. And the operations team could see where the bottlenecks are in the production process to target improvement projects.

For a product, a digital twin would use data captured during its use and collate this for analysis. As an example, an engine in a motorbike could relay real-time temperature and speed information to the manufacturer, who could analyse the data and advise the customer when it's time for a service or to pre-empt issues before they occur. In addition, the data from all the engines in operation could be amalgamated to provide insights into how they are used in service and how they could be improved.

How Do I Do It?

The important part of a digital twin is the data feed from the real-world object, so the first step is to identify what data is already collected and what data you would like to be shown, how this can be measured, and how it can be sent to the digital twin software.

Next, decide how you'd like the data to be processed, displayed, and analysed. For a building it would make sense to view a 2D layout or a 3D model, with filters to change what data is shown, such as the number of people in each room, or which machines are running. It could also have controls to change lighting, heating, and interact with other settings in the building management system or production control systems for example. Add to the requirements list the software and systems that the digital twin will need to share data with, so that these can be accounted for ('Requirements Capture – Hardware' section to 'Requirements Capture – Software' section).

Once you have a requirements document covering these areas, investigate software developers and request proposals from them. It's important to understand if they have any experience creating a solution like this and the feasibility of interacting with the other sources of data such as sensors on the product or building and the control systems used. There's a strong link to the industrial internet of things (IIoT) (see 'Industrial Internet of Things' section) so it would be worth discussing the requirements with an IIoT provider, especially the data collection and transmission side of the project, which a software developer may not be familiar with.

What Are the Benefits and Limitations?

- ✓ Clear presentation of live data from a product or building to improve its performance.
- ✓ Reduced operating costs by identifying unused areas in a building or unused functions on a product range.
- ✓ Increased amount of representative data to help with research and development of products.
- – Solutions will require customisation and will need a number of connections to different systems and sensors, ensure the software developer has experience of this and use the requirements document to clearly describe your needs.

Useful Search Terms

- Digital twin software developer in <<*location*>>.
- IIoT providers in <<*location*>> or <<*industry*>>.

FACTORY SIMULATION, PROCESS SIMULATION, AND HUMAN FACTORS SIMULATION

What Is It?

It is creating a digital copy of some or all of your factory allowing you to simulate how it is likely to operate under certain conditions. This means that you can test what could happen if you make different improvements or changes, allowing you to pick the one which will provide the most benefit, before committing to expensive building work, investing in new equipment, or putting a new shift pattern in place.

With simulations, it's tempting to think of a full virtual reality (VR) model in 3D that you can look around and see the individual parts of your factory in operation, and while this is technically possible, the main aim is to use logic and probabilities to help with decision-making – how the model looks isn't always important. In its simplest form a spreadsheet can be used to create a model, for example, to show how different order levels coming into the factory will affect the load in each production area and what would happen if capacity was increased in one area and not another.

When modelling a full business or factory, discrete event simulation is most appropriate. This takes the processes involved step by step and logically moves orders and parts according to set rules. When set up, inputs to the model include probabilities and logic such as the method of manufacture, operation times, machine capacity, shift patterns, seasonal variation in orders, and scrap rates. The model is run thousands of times to estimate the most likely outcome for any given scenario to see which performs the best.

Process simulation is used at a lower level, such as a group of operations or a chemical process where liquids move continuously between machines, rather than step by step. This is less about probabilities and more about how different parts of the system are connected and work together.

Human factors simulation is used to assess a single operation or task that a person completes. The aim is to ensure that the workplace is designed to be comfortable as well as efficient. An example would be assembling a product by hand using multiple tools and components, a simulation would inform things like which tools need to be closer to the operator or which layout is most ergonomic.

How Do I Do It?

The first step is to decide on the boundaries of the simulation – what's included and what isn't – to avoid creating a model which is too complicated or would take too long to create. A good place to start is by looking at data from business process maps ('Process Map' section) or methods of manufacture to identify which areas would benefit from simulation. This will determine the type of modelling required. It is also useful to write down the aims of the simulation, such as which options you want to simulate and which metrics you'll use to assess them against.

A number of software platforms are available to create your own model, or providers can create the model for you. Allow time for training if doing it in-house and validating the model against real life is important to ensure accuracy.

What Are the Benefits and Limitations?

- ✓ Reduce risk before committing to large projects.
- ✓ Virtually test options and evaluate benefits.
- ✓ Providers can create models for you and capture the data themselves.
- – Models can become complex quickly and require training to get the most benefit, ensure to discuss this with any providers to understand the level of involvement from your team.
- – Outlay could be expensive for something "intangible", create a business case (see 'Business Case' section) to quantify the benefits and explain any avoided costs from reduced risks.

Useful Search Terms

- Factory model in <<*industry*>>.
- Simulation of <<*production process*>>.

SMART GLASSES

What Is It?

These are glasses which have a built-in camera, microphone, and a screen. This means that it's possible to record what the wearer is seeing and hearing, as well as provide them with written instructions, videos, or drawings to enable them to perform a task better while keeping both hands free. Some potential uses for a manufacturing company are:

- Remote assistance. Using smart glasses the wearer is able to join video calls and the camera on the glasses means that the other people on the call can see what the wearer is seeing. The technology means that an experienced technician could stay in the office while supporting a number of trainee technicians, each of them at different sites or locations. If the technicians were servicing or installing products off site, when they needed support the trainer could dial into a video call with them, check the wiring or oversee a task being performed, and advise them of any corrections needed. This would reduce the amount of travel required and also increase the capacity of the trainer to perform other tasks or train more staff in parallel.

- Accessible work instructions. The screen on the smart glasses is able to display checklists, work instructions, drawings, videos, or animations, showing how a task should be performed. While this is possible on a paper copy, tablet screen, or a mobile phone, sometimes this isn't practical. In circumstances where the operator needs both hands free or is working in a difficult to access area, smart glasses provide an effective solution. The operator controls the glasses using voice recognition, cycling through the work instruction as needed while being able to concentrate on the task. Software is available which provides a checklist along with the instructions, so the operator can tick them off as they are completed. This information is then sent to a central system which provides traceability for the tasks.

- Product demonstrations or customer support. Similar to the remote assistance, using the glasses on a video call could help to show potential customers how a product works, advise them on how best to use them, or if the customer has the glasses, they could be used for problem-solving as an alternative to a specialist travelling to the customer's site.

How Do I Do It?

Smart glasses are an accessible technology. The cost of which is similar to a standard mobile phone or tablet, and can be used for video calls without any additional software costs. For them to be used as instructional guides or training aids, there will be additional costs for software subscriptions, so ensure this is considered in the budget when developing the business case; compare it to typical travel costs, cost of scrap, or the additional value of tasks a specialist could be performing.

Start by defining what the use of the smart glasses will be, and capture this in a list of requirements ('Requirements Capture – Software' section). Consider the quality of the screen and camera, the comfort, unit weight, battery life, and interaction with any other software systems such as video calls or job tracking software. There are also options for the screen position; some will project the screen directly in the wearer's line of sight, similar to augmented reality (AR) headsets, while others have a screen which is positioned to the side so the wearer has an unobstructed view of what they're doing.

For tasks other than basic video calls, the software will be the defining element, look for software which can perform the required tasks and then check which hardware is compatible with it.

What Are the Benefits and Limitations?

✓ An accessible technology to help with remote assistance, reducing travel costs, improving productivity, and reducing response times.

✓ More engaging training, providing clear instructions while allowing the wearer to have both hands free.

– For remote tasks, a data connection will be required, consider a 4G dongle or create a Wi-Fi hotspot with a mobile phone to ensure connectivity.

Useful Search Terms

- Industrial smart glasses.
- Remote assistance software for <<*industry or task*>>.

VIRTUAL REALITY (VR)

What Is It?

It is a computer-generated 3D environment which allows the user to explore and interact with objects in a fully immersive way, which means the real world around them isn't visible. This requires the user to wear a headset containing a screen for each eye to create the 3D images, as well as speakers, microphones, and usually hand controllers to coordinate the movements. Alternatively, power walls or VR caves can be used, which project the models onto one or more walls of a room allowing multiple people to interact and view the model at the same time. In this case the headsets are much lighter, as they're only used to create the 3D effect and sometimes to track the wearer's head movements. Example uses in manufacturing are:

- Immersive training. Having a virtual environment allows people to experience unfamiliar or difficult to access environments more easily, so that they're prepared for them in a controlled manner. For example, if a product was designed to be used in hazardous environments, such as in space, in toxic areas, or in difficult to access areas like the Arctic, deep sea, or offshore wind farms. Using VR the operator could practice operating the product, in various scenarios, to ensure that when they are using it in the real environment, they are confident they know how to do it. Similarly, this could apply to expensive or one-off products, where there is a risk of costly damage if an operation is performed incorrectly, VR reduces this risk by improving the operator training.

- Sales demonstrations. For a business manufacturing very large products or items which are difficult to transport, a VR sales environment could be created. This would allow the company to attend trade shows or customer's sites and demonstrate the operation of a product without the transportation costs. This also applies to bespoke items, such as fitted kitchens or other building work.

- Design development. When developing complex products, VR allows designers and engineers to review the prototypes in a virtual environment, which could save a significant amount of time and money compared to physical prototypes. It would also allow team members from remote sites to join a design review, to view the same models as their colleagues and discuss improvements, without the travel costs.

How Do I Do It?

It's important to consider what the system will do first, rather than finding a VR headset and then deciding what to do with it. Use process mapping ('Process Map' section), user stories ('User Stories' section), and a requirements document to clearly define the tasks ('Requirements Capture – Hardware' section to 'Requirements Capture – Software' section). The VR environment will need to be created in a 3D CAD package ('Computer Aided Design' section), if your company already uses CAD for product development, it's likely that there is an additional VR module so check the features and what the equipment requirements are. If you don't use CAD already, then you'll need someone to create the models for you, so include this in the requirements. Often, solution providers will be able to produce the models as well as supply the relevant equipment.

VR environments require a large amount of computing power, and while improvements mean more and more can be done in the headset, it's likely that a dedicated PC, laptop, or server will still be needed to run the system, so ensure this is included in any proposals.

What Are the Benefits and Limitations?

✓ For complex products VR can provide a cost-effective method of testing products, iterating designs, training staff, and improving the sales process.

✓ Reduce risks by testing different scenarios so that people are trained and prepared for them in a safe environment.

✓ Most CAD packages offer VR modules, which just require the addition of a headset, so this can be tested relatively easily, if CAD is already in use in the company.

– Users can take time to get used to a VR system, and some can experience travel sickness, this can be reduced by improving the quality of the animation and other techniques, so discuss this with the service provider.

– Some VR systems go unused in companies for a number of reasons, to avoid this clearly map out what you want to use it for and use demonstrations or trial devices to ensure your staff are engaged and that you find the right solution.

Useful Search Terms

• VR module for <<CAD software>>.
• VR solution providers in <<location or industry>>.

NOTES

1 International Organization for Standardization. (July 2021). *Additive manufacturing general principles fundamentals and vocabulary.* (ISO standard No. 52900:2021). www.iso.org/standard/74514.html

2 *How cyber attacks work.* National Cyber Security Centre. (June 2023). www.ncsc.gov.uk/information/how-cyber-attacks-work

3 International Organization for Standardization. (June 2023). *Quality management systems requirements.* (ISO standard No. 9001:2015). www.iso.org/standard/62085.html

4 *Shared access licences.* Ofcom. (July 2023). www.ofcom.org.uk/manage-your-licence/radiocommunication-licences/shared-access

BIBLIOGRAPHY

All3DP.com. *The 7 main types of 3D printing technology.* July 2023. Available at: https://all3dp.com/1/types-of-3d-printers-3d-printing-technology/

Braincube. *AI vs machine learning vs data science for industry.* July 2023. Available at https://braincube.com/resource/manufacturing-ai-vs-machine-learning-vs-datascience/

International Organization for Standardization. *Additive manufacturing general principles fundamentals and vocabulary.* (ISO standard No. 52900:2021). July 2021. Available at www.iso.org/standard/74514.html

International Organization for Standardization. *Quality management systems requirements.* (ISO standard No. 9001:2015). June 2023. Available at www.iso.org/standard/62085.html

Loughborough University. *The 7 categories of additive manufacturing.* July 2023. Available at www.lboro.ac.uk/research/amrg/about/the7categoriesofadditivemanufacturing/

National Cyber Security Centre. *How cyber attacks work.* June 2023. Available at www.ncsc.gov.uk/information/how-cyberattacks-work

Ofcom. *Shared access licences.* July 2023. Available at www.ofcom.org.uk/manage-your-licence/radiocommunication-licences/shared-access

CHAPTER 4

Tools and Techniques

5S

What Is It?

It is a methodology to improve how well a working area operates, by keeping it tidy and ensuring all tools are available and easily accessible for the operator when they need them. Originating in Japan the process is named after the five Japanese words summarising the steps, fortunately, these have been translated into 5 English words,[1] also beginning with S:

- Sort – remove any unused tools or items which aren't needed for the tasks in that workspace.
- Straighten – organise the workspace so that the remaining tools are all stored where they're easily accessible, working to the mantra "a place for everything, and everything in its place".
- Shine – clean the entire workspace, to give an ideal starting point or baseline that can always be returned to.
- Standardise – agree and write the operating procedures and cleaning schedules for the space to ensure it is maintained. Often this is taking

DOI: 10.1201/9781032642215-5

a photo after the shine step to easily show the standard as part of visual management.

- Sustain – make the process successful by reinforcing the workplace procedures defined in the standardise step, and maintain the focus.

How Do I Do It?

The 5S technique can be used in either the shop floor or office, but it's important to start with a small area first to get used to how it works and to make it manageable to implement.

- Pick one area as a trial, such as a single workbench or cell in the production area, or a group of four desks in one section of the office.
- Explain the principles to the staff that work in the area so that they understand the intent and the benefits.
- Ensure there is enough time to complete the first four steps, and plan production to allow this to happen.
- Work with the team from the area to decide what can be removed, how the remaining items should be organised, to clean the area, and to decide how it should be maintained.
- Be open to feedback about what works and what doesn't, before rolling out the principles to the other areas step by step.

What Are the Benefits and Limitations?

- ✓ More efficient operation in the area from knowing where the important tools are.
- ✓ Improved quality and process understanding.
- – Staff can be sceptical about the benefits, so start with a small area where you learn together, allow the time to complete the process and seeing how it works will help build engagement.
- – It can be hard to throw items away, if the team is unsure about whether to keep an item, store it elsewhere in a quarantine area for an agreed amount of time to see if it gets used, before removing it completely.

Useful Search Terms

- 5S in manufacturing.

DESIGN OF EXPERIMENTS (DOE) AND STATISTICAL ANALYSIS

What Is It?

It is a technique to identify which variables in a process have the most impact on the output quality. It uses a systematic test in which the input variables are adjusted, and the output is carefully monitored. The results of the study identify which process variables are key process variables (KPVs); these are the ones which have the largest effect on quality. Once complete it allows you to put controls in place on the KPVs to make sure the process always operates within the required tolerances to give a satisfactory output.

As an example, in a plastic extrusion process the operator might be able to adjust the temperature of the input plastic, the speed of the extrusion, and the pressure applied to the plastic. There might be other factors which the team think affect the extrusion quality, which are the temperature and humidity of the room, moulding with plastic pellets from different manufacturers, and the cleanliness of the machine. Using the design of experiments (DoE) technique, a series of tests are defined by software, which creates a plan to change these variables within set limits and then measure the quality of the output after each test.

With each variable having two or three levels (high and low, or high, medium, and low), testing all of these variables would require 34 experiments, which may be impractical in a production environment. By reducing the tests to only focus on the speed, temperature, and pellet manufacturer, the number of experiments required drops to less than 10. The results might show that the pellet manufacturers don't have a large effect, but the temperature is the most important, and this is where the tighter controls should be placed.

How Do I Do It?

Select the process which is in need of control, and define the limits of the test. Discuss the potential variables with everyone involved in the process, such as the operators, engineers, designers, or maintenance. Agree the variables to be tested first and define the quality measures to be used on the output. Online tools or statistical software are available to create the test plan, including the sequence of tests and the value of each variable to use.

Conduct the experiments according to the plan, being careful to adhere to the defined values and accurately measuring the output. Once complete, input the results into the software, which will analyse them and provide the results showing which have the most effect and also the scale of the interaction between variables.

Agree with the team how to control the required KPVs, and decide if any further experiments are required to either test other variables or to refine the tolerance limits on the KPVs studied.

What Are the Benefits and Limitations?

✓ Improved understanding of a process, enabling control measures to be put in place.

✓ A systematic approach which will highlight how the process is currently controlled.

– Processes with a high number of variables will need a larger number of tests, selecting the three or four most likely first will help to reduce the number, and if none of these have an effect the results will show it, allowing you to test other variables.

– Each of the variables and outputs need a clear measure or value, which can be difficult to define or some variables could be outside of your control, for example, the weather. Research measures for the variables you're considering or discuss with a specialist.

Useful Search Terms

• Design of experiments online tool.

• Design of experiments software and training.

LEAN MANUFACTURING

What Is It?

It is an approach to continuous improvement in a business through the identification and reduction of waste. There are a large number of tools and techniques involved in lean manufacturing, which can be used individually or applied to different areas of the business. Many companies choose to adopt it as a mindset or a culture within the entire business as the principles can be applied to office processes as well as production.

The reduction of waste in any process should result in improved productivity, process flow, and quality. This will allow the business to become more profitable, accept more orders, and achieve the objectives in the long-term strategy.

There are five principles of lean:[2]

- Specify value – anything which the customer would pay for, everything else is waste. A customer could be the end user of the product or the next operation on the production line.
- Identify the value stream – a value stream map (VSM) of every operation from an order being placed to delivery of the product or service.
- Flow – creating a method where products move through the operations in the most efficient manner, the ultimate being one-piece flow – each operation produces one a part at a time before handing it to the next operation.
- Pull – demand is driven directly from the customer requirement. This demand for a product cascades backwards through the production line, by each process signalling in turn that it needs feeding from the preceding operation.
- Perfection – the first four principles will continue to highlight waste in the system, and the final one is to strive for perfection by removing this waste.

How Do I Do It?

In some industries it will be difficult to fully apply these principles, but the key to identifying improvements is to look for the eight types of waste created in any process, and this concept is universal:

- Overproduction – making products that aren't required.
- Overprocessing – performing operations or tasks which don't add value.
- Transportation – moving products around doesn't add value and should be reduced.
- Inventory – any stock over the minimum requirement.
- Motion – any movement of people should be reduced.
- Waiting – products, people, or machines not being used.
- Defects – scrap or rework on any products.
- People – the unused potential of staff and the ideas they may have.

As a starting point, pick a single area and talk the staff through the eight wastes, before using a checklist to go through their processes step by step, identifying waste in each one. Encourage the team to think of improvements to reduce the causes of waste. VSMs ('Value Stream Map' section) are a useful tool to spot waste in the business as a whole. Once you have the improvement ideas, use a plan, do, check, act cycle to embed or develop the improvement ideas.

What Are the Benefits and Limitations?

✓ Produces a focus on continuous improvement, resulting in more efficient processes.

✓ Simple to get started in any area of the business.

– The one-piece flow and customer pull concepts aren't suitable for every type of manufacturing process or company, but the individual tools of lean will still be beneficial.

– Some concepts can be counterintuitive, ensure the team understand why they are being used, and encourage an open dialogue where concerns or ideas can be raised and discussed.

Useful Search Terms

- Lean manufacturing training in <<*location*>>.
- Lean manufacturing tools and techniques.

OVERALL EQUIPMENT EFFECTIVENESS (OEE)

What Is It?

It is an indicator of how well a machine is performing by measuring its availability, performance, and quality of the products it produces. There is a calculation which combines these elements into a single OEE score, displayed as a percentage. When the OEE for each machine is shown side by side it makes it easier for the production and maintenance teams to see which machines need improvement.

A machine operating at 100% OEE is producing parts for the entire time it's planned to be running, with perfect quality. If the machine is down for planned or unplanned maintenance, perhaps by two hours in a ten-hour shift, its availability is 80%. If it operates slower than planned, producing 10% fewer parts, then its performance reduces to 90%. And if the quality of the parts means 70% are acceptable, that's its quality score. The combined OEE figure for that machine is 80% × 90% × 70% = 50.4%, showing that it only made just over half the parts that it could have if it was working to its full capability.

The elements which can affect each metric are:

- Availability – no work for the machine to do, planned downtime, unplanned downtime, and setup time.
- Performance – speed reduction and minor stoppages.
- Quality – defects and rework.

How Do I Do It?

The data for the OEE calculations can either be gathered manually, by asking operators to fill in a chart each hour to account for what the machine is doing, or it can be collected automatically from the machine's programmable logic controller (PLC) where this is available. Using the manual method can be effective for a short-term investigation into a machine's productivity, as long as the shop floor staff understand why they need to collect the data and its importance.

For long-term solutions, it's worth investigating how the data collection can be automated, and this should include the analysis and reporting elements. Solutions are available for machines without a PLC using retrofitted sensors ('Industrial Internet of Things' section), as well as those with a PLC where software solutions can gather the information automatically from the machine.

What Are the Benefits and Limitations?

- ✓ Improved machine performance, quality, and availability.
- ✓ Improved process understanding and increased capacity.
- – Applying all three categories to a particular process can be difficult, such as getting a quality measure to feed into the calculation, so apply the elements which are most appropriate. In a lot of cases the machine availability or performance is the priority.

Useful Search Terms

- OEE system for <<*manufacturing process*>>.
- OEE data collection for <<*machine type*>>.

- Machine monitoring and reporting system for <<*industry*>>.

PROCESS INPUT/OUTPUT DIAGRAM

What Is It?

It is a diagram showing the input and output variables of a process, along with the resources required and control methods, to help with identifying improvements or communicating the details to suppliers and third parties. They are particularly useful when defining a new piece of equipment as it shows exactly what needs to be controlled for the process to be effective.

The diagram has the process in the centre as a black box, because the aim is to describe what the process needs to do without prescribing how it should to do it (see Figure 4.1). The inputs to the black box are:

- Output from the previous operation, in a baking process this would be the prepared cake mix.
- Additional material required – this would be the greaseproof paper and butter for the tin.
- Data required – this would be the recipe number and order number.

The diagram also details what is needed during the process:

- The controls, or key process variables (KPVs) ('Key Process Variables' section') – this would be the baking time and temperature.
- The enablers – this would be the operator, cake tins, and the appropriate work instructions.

Finally, the diagram shows the outputs:

- The product that the process creates, in the baking example this would be the cake.
- Material outputs – this would be the spillages or any cakes which didn't bake properly.
- Data generated – this would be actual time and temperatures for traceability and the batch number.

Example input / output diagram

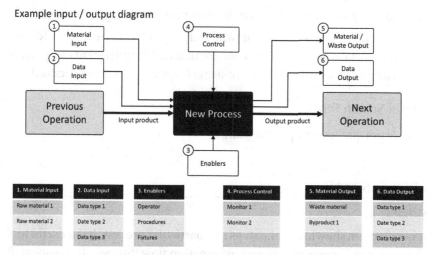

FIGURE 4.1   An example of a process input/output diagram.

How Do I Do It?

Observing the operation first hand is a good starting point, as this will allow you to see things like the input material, any materials required, and what data is used, and then similarly for the outputs. Start to complete the diagram as you notice things; it can always be refined later on.

It might be possible to complete the KPVs from experience, but performing a design of experiments (DoE) ('Design of Experiments' section) will give a more reliable answer.

If you are creating a specification for a new process, use the process map ('Process Map' section) or method of manufacture details as a starting point, and build up the remaining information systematically from any initial trials or by observing similar operations. If the machine needs to interact with any other systems, such as manufacturing execution systems (MES) ('Shop Floor Data Capture' section), order tracking software ('Order Tracking' section), or machine monitoring ('Industrial Internet of Things' section), then it's important to include these details in the data section of the diagram.

There is a template and example in the resources section of the website.

What Are the Benefits and Limitations?

✓ Clearly describes a process and its requirements when specifying a new machine or system.

✓ Identify any knowledge gaps in your understanding of the process.

– The information provided will only be an overview, so add further details in a requirements document ('Requirements Capture – Hardware' section to 'Requirements Capture – Software' section).

Useful Search Terms

• Input-process-output diagram.

PROCESS MAP

What Is It?

It is a diagram showing all the steps in a particular process. It is a useful tool to understand how products and information flow through the business. It is used to identify where to focus improvement projects and also to capture company procedures when investigating software tools so you can be sure the software will be a good fit. See Figure 4.2 for a simple example of a process map.

How Do I Do It?

Creating a process map should be a team effort, make sure to involve people who actually do the tasks to capture the process correctly.

• Set the boundaries of the map you're going to create – you could choose to focus on one particular product as it travels from design through manufacturing to dispatch, or you could choose to focus on a particular area such as sales or inspection. Agreeing this now will make the task more manageable and make it more likely to be finished. It can be easier to create a high-level map of the whole business, and then take one area at a time to add more detail.

• With the correct people involved, start to list the high-level activities involved in the area you're focusing on. Walking the production process or following an actual product/order as it progresses through the area are good ways to understand what actually happens. Sticky notes, flipcharts, or just large sheets of paper work perfectly well for this process. Common desktop software for spreadsheets, creating diagrams, or presentations can be used, and there are free or low-cost processing mapping software solutions available online.

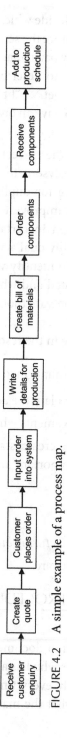

FIGURE 4.2 A simple example of a process map.

- From the list of activities decide which is the starting point, and work through step by step to capture the sequence, accurately showing what needs to happen before any particular task can start. Each task should be an action, so use verbs to describe them – such as "input order details", "inspect weld geometry", "fit accessories", or "print shipping label". Each activity should have an output that is passed onto the next activity.

- Once the activities are in the correct order, the process map is now a useful tool. You can analyse it to find where the process can be improved, such as looking for duplication which can be removed, or adjusting the order to improve the flow. It may be more useful to add further information in certain parts. For example, adding times for how long the individual activities should take or how long they actually take can help identify which ones need improving. Or adding where data is created and where it is used can help to scope requirements for a new software tool.

There is a template and example in the resources section of the website.

What Are the Benefits and Limitations?

- ✓ Clearly understand and explain the activities within the business.
- ✓ Identify and target improvements where they're most needed.
- – Can be time consuming to create, start with a high-level overview of the business, then map important areas or processes in manageable sections.

Useful Search Terms

- Process map for <<*manufacturing business or process*>>.
- Free process mapping software.

STANDARD OPERATING PROCEDURE (SOP)

What Is It?

It is a straightforward instruction document which shows the steps in an operation, allowing an operator who has already been trained on the operation to perform it consistently every time. It provides a clear reminder of which tools are required, what the machine settings are, and what the sequence of tasks are. It is useful when there are a number of different products going through the same cell or machine, but with variations in how they are processed.

For example, a company making pasta of different shapes would use SOPs to make sure the operators select the correct tools and settings. When the production schedule shows they needed to make spaghetti, they could refer to the spaghetti SOP, which would tell them to fit the spaghetti die to the machine and which extrusion speed to set the machine to, along with any other important steps or settings. When changing to penne pasta shapes, the operator would find the penne SOP so they could be sure they were fitting the correct die and selecting the correct machine settings.

How Do I Do It?

Observe the process first hand, noting the order that the tasks are completed, which tools are used, and what the machine settings are. Take photos of the tools and key steps so they can be added to the SOP. Asking the operator to describe what they're doing and why will help to capture the key points.

When writing the SOP it's important to remember that it isn't a training manual, each step should have a short description and a clear drawing or photo to serve as reference. The operator will be using this while performing the tasks so it should be detailed enough to remind them what to do, but short enough that it allows them to concentrate on the operation.

Once the first version is written, ask different operators for feedback. This may draw out variations in how the operators perform the tasks, and allow the team to agree on the standard method. When the version is agreed, it should be issued to the shop floor and placed somewhere accessible to ensure they get used – either laminated paper copies to avoid them getting damaged, or on a tablet or screen at the workstation.

There is a template and example in the resources section of the website.

What Are the Benefits and Limitations?

- ✓ Improved quality and consistency of production by standardising operations and providing a reference to operators.
- ✓ Identify variations in how operations are performed, allowing you to select the most effective.

- It can be difficult to convince confident operators to refer to the SOP, making sure they're involved in the process and making the SOP accessible and quick to use will make this easier.
- Creating SOPs for every process and every product type can be time consuming, prioritise the most critical operations and group products where variations are minor.

Useful Search Terms

- Standard operation procedure.
- SOP in manufacturing.

VALUE STREAM MAP (VSM)

What Is It?

It is a diagram showing how the material flows from start to finish in a production process, with the addition of information flows, cycle times, and lead times for each stage. The idea is to highlight where waste occurs and where improvements can be made by laying out the entire process on a single diagram.

A VSM differs from a process map as it has much more detailed information. The starting point is the material arriving from the supplier and finishes with the end product being delivered to the customer. From an information flow perspective this includes the order frequency from the customer, how often production plans are communicated, and which parts of the process this information goes to. Once complete, it's easy to see the comparison between the lead time of the products and the actual time taken to create them, as well as how long products spend waiting in storage or how long operations take. This holistic view of the production process allows the team to focus improvement efforts where they will have the most impact.

How Do I Do It?

The first step is to decide which product will be the focus of the VSM; this maybe the highest volume product your company makes, the most representative of your product range, or the one needing improvement the most. Then define the limits, usually this will be from the raw material arriving from your suppliers through to delivery to the customer, but in some cases it is worthwhile including the entire supply chain in a higher-level map if there are external issues. Before starting to create the VSM, make sure to have the right expertise involved. This is a team activity, as it's unlikely that any one person will have the knowledge and access to the data required to complete it in the necessary detail.

The starting point is a process map, a method of manufacture, or an operation list for the product. Make a box for each step of the process in a diagramming software package or on a large piece of paper, and add arrows to show the flow of the material. The information flow from customers and to suppliers should then be overlayed to show how data is shared. Start to add the cycle times and queue times, researching from software systems or timing them where the data isn't available – using accurate data makes the process much more effective.

Analyse the completed diagram to identify what can be done to resolve the key issues, such as long lead times, capacity constraints, or production bottlenecks. Define the actions required to reduce the waste in the system, and in some cases creating an ideal state VSM is useful to highlight what is possible.

What Are the Benefits and Limitations?

✓ Provides a holistic view of the production process, highlighting areas of waste and non-value add processes (see 'Lean Manufacturing' section).

✓ Shows the difference between lead time and value add time allowing identification of areas that require improvement.

✓ Creating it as a team improves understanding of the different areas of the business.

– Requires a large amount of data, some of which won't be available immediately and will require investigation. Allow the team time to create the full diagram, while it might be easy to create the outline in a single session, the value comes from adding the detail.

Useful Search Terms

- Online VSM tools.
- Diagramming software or online diagramming tools.

PROJECT MANAGEMENT

What Is It?

It is the process of leading and delivering a project by controlling the activities, resources, money, and risks associated with it. This section refers to traditional project management which is used for projects with a fixed goal or a lot of sequential steps which need to happen in a certain order, for example, the construction of a new manufacturing building, an extension to a production facility, or the production of a complex machine. For projects where the timescales are difficult to predict or the requirements are likely to change, such as developing a new software program, see agile project management ('Agile Project Management' section).

Formalising how projects are managed within a business could be a requirement from a key customer, in particular if your business is part of a complex supply chain, or it could just be a way of maintaining focus on projects which aren't related to the day-to-day production requirements. The subject is wide ranging and is covered in many books, training courses, and degree programs, but as an introduction some important elements are:

- Understanding the requirements of the project – agreeing what needs to be delivered and by whom, what the budget is, and what the timescales are.
- Stakeholder analysis – who needs to be involved in the project, who needs to be aware of the progress, who can affect the success of the project, and how to manage the communication to them all.
- Risk analysis and management – identifying things which could affect the outcome of the project or particular tasks, either positively or negatively, and putting actions in place to reduce the negative impact or maximise the positive impact. See 'Risk Management' section.
- Scheduling – deciding what activities need to happen in order to deliver the project, what sequence they need to happen in, how long they'll take, and what resources they'll need. See 'Network Diagram' section and 'Gantt Chart' section
- Change control – keeping track of anything which affects the defined cost, time, or quality of the project or activities within the project, and agreeing these changes with the stakeholders.

How Do I Do It?

Establish a project management process within your business which allows staff the time to work on any special projects which aren't related to the normal daily production operations. At a simple level this would be a governance meeting where each project manager has the opportunity to update the leadership team on progress, highlight any risks, and request guidance on key decisions. For important projects this could occur weekly or fortnightly, and for lower priority projects it could be monthly.

At the start of each project the scope should be agreed. This includes:

- What needs to be delivered and by when.
- What is in scope and what's out of scope.
- A definition of the resource available, and how much time the project manager should spend running the project.
- How often the project manager needs to report on progress.

What Are the Benefits and Limitations?

✓ Improved success of unusual tasks which aren't related to the company's normal operation.

✓ Clearer role definitions for staff responsible for these tasks, with better control of budgets.

✓ Compliance with project management requirements defined by larger customers.

– It can be viewed as a non-value add activity, but with the correct governance and giving project managers autonomy, it can free up the leadership team's time while keeping them informed with progress.

Useful Search Terms

- Project management courses in <<*location*>>.
- Traditional project management vs agile project management.
- Association of Project Management resources.[3]

AGILE PROJECT MANAGEMENT

What Is It?

It is the process of leading and delivering a project by controlling the activities, resources, money, and risks associated with it. This section refers to agile project management[4] which is used for projects where the timescales are difficult to predict or the requirements are likely to change, such as developing a new software program, or developing a new product where prototypes can be produced and tested quickly. For projects where there is a fixed goal or a lot of sequential steps which need to happen in a certain order, see 'Project Management' section.

The key element of agile project management is establishing a vision or an aim for the project, once that is done there will be a number of iterations of solutions to the problem, with a focus on improving each attempt to get closer to the vision. The focus is on speed and constantly responding to feedback or changes in requirements. This is achieved with high levels of collaboration and empowering teams to solve problems on their own.

The sprint methodology is used as an approach to managing projects in an agile manner. At the start of the project the length of each sprint is agreed, usually one or two weeks. Each sprint begins with a review of the results of the last sprint, any updates to the requirements, feedback from testing, and then a commitment from the team on what they will achieve during the next sprint. The aim is to deliver results quickly, in software this is a minimum viable product (MVP) – something that has just enough features to prove the concept and encourage users, allowing the team to get feedback, refine the product, and add more features.

How Do I Do It?

Agile project management often requires a different way of thinking about developing a product, and so it's important to discuss the approach with staff first, and explain why you want to do it and what the benefits will be to the company and to them.

Pick a small pilot project to try the collaborative approach and sprint methodology, agree how long each sprint will be, and who will be involved from each area of the business. Use tools such as user stories ('User Stories' section) to understand the requirements of the product, and allow the team the autonomy to develop solutions to the user's issues on their own.

Commit to reviewing how the process is working after each sprint and aim for a continuous improvement approach to refine and develop how the process works for you.

What Are the Benefits and Limitations?

✓ Reduced time to market.

✓ Improved collaboration and staff autonomy.

✓ Increased focus on the user requirements and developing specific solutions.

- Staff training, and potentially a culture change may be required, make sure to involve staff all the way through and commit to implementing the process.
- If customers use the traditional project management approach, then communicating progress will be more difficult, for example, dates for key milestones could be vague or detailed project plans won't be created, so discuss these requirements and your approach with the customer.

Useful Search Terms

- Agile project management in manufacturing.
- Agile project management vs traditional project management.
- Agile or scrum/scrum master training in <<*location*>> or online.

NETWORK DIAGRAM

What Is It?

It is a tool used to identify the individual tasks required to complete a project, along with how long each one will take, and the order they need to be completed in. A network diagram is used in the planning phase of the project when using a traditional project management approach ('Project Management' section) and provides the information needed to create a Gantt chart. It's an often-overlooked step when starting a project, as it's tempting to go straight into working out how long the entire project will take. The benefit of creating a network diagram is that it allows a team to get together and discuss each phase of the project, decide what needs to happen, and it usually draws out required tasks which hadn't been considered before.

How Do I Do It?

The process works best when completed as a team, with a representative from each function, such as sales, manufacturing, design, finance, and logistics. Use an online diagramming tool or a pile of sticky notes – something which can easily be moved around as the team discusses what needs to happen. See Figure 4.3 for an example.

- List the obvious tasks that each person thinks will be required to deliver the project.

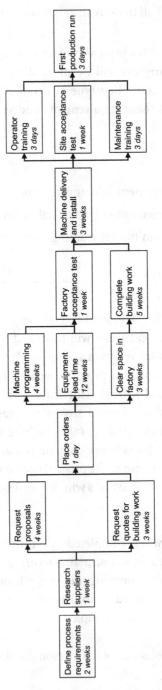

FIGURE 4.3   An example of a network diagram.

- Organise them into the order they need to happen.
- Draw arrows connecting the activities to show dependencies, that is which tasks need to be completed before it's possible to start another.
- Review the sequence of tasks looking for any missing dependencies or activities which need to be included. Working both forwards and backwards through the diagram is a good way to tease out any missing tasks, asking what is needed to allow any particular task to start.
- Add in an estimate for how long each task will take.

At this point project management software is able to calculate the total duration of the project, as well as output dates like the earliest start or the latest finish for each task. This helps to manage tasks around resource availability without affecting the final delivery date. It would also show the critical path, which is the sequence of tasks which don't have any flexibility in when they're completed, usually referred to as tasks without any slack or float.

What Are the Benefits and Limitations?

- ✓ A reliable method of identifying what needs to happen in a project and in what order.
- ✓ Improved awareness of activities across the different functions of the business.
- ✓ Leads to a more accurate and usable Gantt chart.
- − It can be unwieldy for large projects, but it can be done in sections if each element is treated as a project in its own right.

Useful Search Terms

- Free online diagramming tools.
- Project management software.

GANTT CHART

What Is It?

It is a diagram showing the tasks required to complete a project, how long they will take, and the date when the project will finish. It's an overview of the timeline or timescales of a project, but it can be useful to include additional information such as:

- Who is responsible for each task.
- What are the links or dependencies between tasks, which need to be done before others can start.
- Important or key milestones which need to be met, such as delivery of a prototype to the customer.
- Current progress against the original plan – how much of each task is complete.
- Highlighting the critical path, which is the sequence of tasks which must be completed on time in order to meet the completion date.

The Gantt chart is normally created in the planning phase of a project, when using traditional project management techniques ('Project Management' section). It's used as a baseline or a reference point to communicate with customers, suppliers, or other people in the business explaining when they can expect things to happen, and who will be doing them. A Gantt chart can also be helpful when planning the workload of people in the team or when machines or other resources will be required, as it clearly shows the dates and the current progress. See Figure 4.4 for an example.

How Do I Do It?

There are many Gantt chart templates available online to be used with desktop spreadsheet software, or there are a number of dedicated project management software tools which provide Gantt chart functions. Whichever tool you choose to use, when you create a Gantt chart it shouldn't be the first time you write down the tasks involved in a project. This is because it's easy to focus on the main tasks required, which often means that dependencies or minor tasks are missed.

The starting point should be a network diagram ('Network Diagram' section) which helps you work out all the tasks in a project, how long they'll take, and in what order they can be done. This makes the creation of the Gantt chart much simpler, and also will make it clearer for other people to understand as it can be laid out in a logical sequence rather than the order the tasks come to mind.

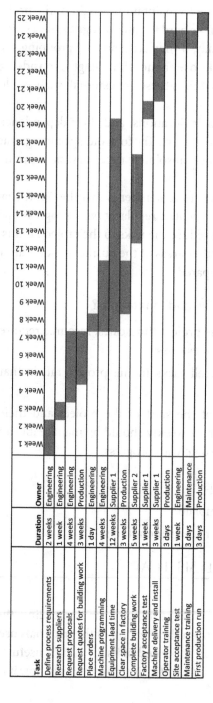

Task	Duration	Owner	Week 1	Week 2	Week 3	Week 4	Week 5	Week 6	Week 7	Week 8	Week 9	Week 10	Week 11	Week 12	Week 13	Week 14	Week 15	Week 16	Week 17	Week 18	Week 19	Week 20	Week 21	Week 22	Week 23	Week 24	Week 25
Define process requirements	2 weeks	Engineering																									
Research suppliers	1 week	Engineering																									
Request proposals	4 weeks	Engineering																									
Request quotes for building work	3 weeks	Production																									
Place orders	1 day	Engineering																									
Machine programming	4 weeks	Engineering																									
Equipment lead time	12 weeks	Supplier 1																									
Clear space in factory	3 weeks	Production																									
Complete building work	5 weeks	Supplier 2																									
Factory acceptance test	1 week	Supplier 1																									
Machine delivery and install	3 weeks	Supplier 1																									
Operator training	3 days	Production																									
Site acceptance test	1 week	Engineering																									
Maintenance training	3 days	Maintenance																									
First production run	3 days	Production																									

FIGURE 4.4   An example of a Gantt chart.

Consider the level of detail your Gantt chart needs, if it's very detailed it will take a lot of time to maintain throughout the project, and if it's not detailed enough it will be hard to gauge progress. As a guide, tasks shouldn't be shorter than one day, if they are, consider grouping some together into a longer task. For tasks over a month in length, consider splitting them up to give more control, unless these are external, such as a long lead time on a new machine.

Input the tasks, their durations, and their dependencies, and this will automatically create the chart. Try to avoid specifying exact dates for tasks to start and finish, unless absolutely necessary, as this removes flexibility in the project.

The important thing to remember is that the Gantt chart is a live document – it should be updated regularly with progress and any additional tasks which will help reduce the risks to the project. If it is updated weekly, when customers or other areas of the business ask for an update, the information is already prepared.

What Are the Benefits and Limitations?

✓ Easy to visualise project timescales, resource requirements, and progress towards milestones.

✓ Keeps track of all tasks in the project rather than just the high-profile ones.

– Often created at the start of the project and then left untouched, updating the chart weekly should be manageable and will help keep everyone up to date with progress.

Useful Search Terms

- Gantt chart template.
- Online project management tools.

LIFE CYCLE ANALYSIS (LCA)

What Is It?

It is a method of investigating and understanding the environmental impact of a product from the creation of the materials used through to the disposal of the product at the end of its life. This is useful to understand the impact of a product and identify improvements in how it is produced, used, and disposed of. This allows the impact to be reduced, as well as identifying ways to simplify the supply chains, make them more resilient, and potentially reduce costs and lead times.

Performing a LCA on a product is useful in understanding the contribution a particular product makes to the company's scope 3 emissions ('Net Zero' section), and will allow the company to identify actions to make the product more sustainable and enable the circular economy. It will also help the company to comply with environmental regulations and identify improvements to future products.

For example, a company that makes a range of wooden furniture would have a good understanding of what is involved in the production of each product. By conducting an LCA on one of their chairs, they would consider elements such as:

- Where the wood is sourced from, how sustainable it is, how it is processed, and transported to them.
- Where additional items come from, such as the source of metallic fixings like screws and where the raw material is mined and processed, or what type of plastic is used for the washers and where these are processed and what content is recycled.
- The energy used in the production of the chair in the factory, as well as any other by-products such as wastewater, emissions, or chemicals.
- How much waste is generated from the factory and if this is recycled, reused, or disposed of, for example.
- How the finished chair is packaged, distributed to warehouses and customers.
- How easy the chair is to disassemble when it is no longer required, if the raw material can be separated and reused or recycled.

How Do I Do It?

There are online tools to help with LCA, or there are companies offering it as a service, which may be beneficial for complex products.

Start by agreeing the scope of the assessment – which product will be the focus and what are the boundaries of the study. In the chair example above, it might be decided that the plastic washers don't need to be included because the supplier has already provided an in-depth analysis or maybe they won't be included in future versions of the design.

Detail the bill of materials, where each is sourced from and how much is required to make the product, including any waste. The online calculators will guide you through the process of calculating the impact, either from a database of common products or by calculating an estimate using averages from different types of industry. Similarly, calculate the impacts from the distribution of your completed product, any caused during its service life, and how it is broken up and processed when it is disposed of.

What Are the Benefits and Limitations?

✓ A detailed understanding of the environmental impact of a product, allowing improvements to be identified and compliance with regulations.

✓ A significant step towards understanding your scope 3 emissions, helping with the plan to reach net zero emissions.

– An in-depth study which will take time and resources, so prioritise the key products in your portfolio, and allow the time to complete the study properly.

Useful Search Terms

- LCA tools.
- LCA in <<*industry*>>.
- LCA consultant or specialist in <<*industry or location*>>.

RISK MANAGEMENT

What Is It?

It is the process of identifying events which may affect the delivery of a project, and then putting plans in place to either reduce the likelihood of them happening or reduce the impact of them. This also applies to events which could positively affect the project and looking at how the likelihood can be maximised. For example, if the company is planning to move production into a new building the following events could be identified as potentially happening, and what the team could do to mitigate them:

- If an old machine doesn't work correctly after the move, then production output will be lower than required. To reduce the likelihood of this happening the machine could be serviced before and after the move. And to reduce the impact if it still occurs, they could over produce ahead of the move to build up a buffer stock.

- If a key supplier decides to move their production to the same industrial estate, then logistics will be easier and communication will be improved. The team could discuss their plans with their suppliers and consider the opportunities of having facilities nearby, in an attempt to make it more likely.

Companies dealing with larger organisations in complex supply chains could be asked to perform regular risk reviews where the team go through the tasks in a project plan and identify events which have the potential to affect the project, before scoring them by likelihood and impact. The highest scoring risks should have actions added to the plan which will attempt to reduce the probability of them happening or the effect on the project if they do. This would be managed in a risk register, which is a list of all the identified risks, their associated scores, and what actions have been put in place to manage them.

How Do I Do It?

Identifying risks works best when it is done as a team, so that each element can be discussed and evaluated. The process should be performed regularly so that any new risks can be addressed as the project progresses. The most important part is making sure that actions are put in place to manage the risks.

- Risk management should start at the beginning of the project and think about what could happen which may affect the project scope, budget, or timescales. Keep a log of the risks and what could be done to help.
- As the project progresses review the risks and go through the tasks in the project plan thinking about anything that could affect those individual items. If there are a large number, it's worth scoring the likelihood and effect as a way of making the process more manageable by addressing the highest scores.
- Add any new tasks which address the risks to the project plan, and assign an owner to the each risk and action to make managing them easier.

What Are the Benefits and Limitations?

- ✓ Improve the delivery of a project by addressing events which are likely to have a significant impact on the project.
- ✓ Discussing them as a team raises awareness of people's concerns and improves communication.
- ✓ More likely to comply with requirements from large customers with project management functions.
- – It's impossible to predict everything and it's easy to generate a long list of things that could go wrong, so approach it in a pragmatic way and address the risks which have the highest likelihood of occurring or will have the biggest impact on the project.

Useful Search Terms

- Risk management in <<*industry*>>.
- Guidelines for conducting risk reviews.

TIME MANAGEMENT

What Is It?

It is putting steps in place to improve the productivity of individuals or the team. In many small businesses the leadership team is reliant on one or two people, who find it difficult to dedicate their time to things which don't directly relate to the day-to-day running of the company. Using strategies to manage time will allow headroom to work on developing new products, entering new markets, improving resilience, or implementing new technologies. The approach to organising your days and weeks will vary depending on everything from the type of business through to personal style and preference, but there are two techniques which may be appropriate:

- Standard diary – create a structure for the core meetings to deal with regular tasks at the same time each day. This could include a meeting every morning for 15 minutes to discuss the production plan for the day and review issues facing the team, so that everyone is clear and any issues can be resolved. And then have weekly slots for items which don't need to be reviewed as frequently, such as progress updates for projects or continuous improvement meetings. Giving items like these a dedicated time in the week helps the team to focus on them and give them their full attention, making them less likely to feel like a chore or to be something that never gets addressed through the normal working day.

- Delegation and autonomy – trust the team with more tasks and give them the freedom to work on them in their own way. At first they may need more guidance but as they become more confident this will reduce. Including these additional tasks in their job description will help to make it more formal and increase the chances of success ('Roles and Responsibilities' section). This will also help with succession planning ('Succession Planning' section) and business resilience.

How Do I Do It?

There are a lot of different productivity techniques available, and every person works differently, so it's important to find something that works well for the team and the people in it – some people respond well to structure, others need more flexibility, so be considerate of how each person prefers to work.

- Discuss what you want to get out of the approach to managing time. For example, is the aim to free up time to allow people to focus on a special project, such as introducing a new software package or investigating a new technology.
- Be open to suggestions and be willing to try different approaches for a few weeks to see what works and what doesn't.
- Make sure everyone understands why the approaches are needed and how they should work.
- Try to think who is needed in a particular meeting or who is involved in a task, and if they need to be, if not they should be allowed to leave and work on something that is their priority.

What Are the Benefits and Limitations?

- ✓ More available time to focus on growing the business or on specific projects.

✓ Improved clarity for staff on which tasks they are responsible for.

✓ There are a lot of productivity techniques available, and many are easy to try.

– A technique may not work for everyone, so be aware of people's preferences and work with them to alleviate their concerns.

Useful Search Terms

- Time management techniques or leadership productivity techniques.
- Tools to improve <<*specific time management issue*>>.

REQUIREMENTS CAPTURE – HARDWARE

What Is It?

It is a method of understanding and then defining exactly what a piece of equipment needs to do, and not necessarily how it will do it. This is useful when looking to buy a new machine, as it describes the features you need, explains what the process is to potential suppliers, and clearly shows what needs to be delivered and what doesn't. It also makes it easier for suppliers to create a proposal, allows an objective comparison of different proposals, and makes sure that all the team know what is covered. Some examples of what to include in the requirements document are:

- The number of parts it will have to process in a shift, a week, or any relevant period of time.
- The range of products, the smallest and largest sizes and weights, the number of variants, and how they are processed – for example, the number in a batch or how often products will be changed.
- Material types, surface finish requirements, and tolerances that need to be achieved.
- Relevant health and safety or environmental requirements.
- Process requirements, such as target cycle time or quality rates.
- Data connectivity, such as programming language or other software and systems it needs to connect with.
- Operations and maintenance requirements – how you need your staff to interact with the machine, number of people to be trained, and access levels.

- Acceptance criteria – how you will check that the machine does what it needs to, see ('Acceptance Testing for Equipment' section).

How Do I Do It?

Creating a process map ('Process Map' section) or an input–output diagram ('Input-Output Diagram' section) is a good place to start, as this defines the boundary of the process and gives an overview of what the machine needs to do.

The requirements document doesn't have to be a long and exhaustive account of everything. The process of collating the main requirements is a very good start and will help to focus on the type of machine you need and which suppliers can offer a solution. Include numbers wherever possible as this will give a solution that's a good fit for your production. For example, stating a product is high volume means very different things in different industries, whereas stating you need to produce 200 parts in a shift is specific, and suppliers shouldn't propose a machine that can produce 10,000 in a shift when it's not necessary.

Consider any future plans for the business, the service life of a machine is very long, so ensuring it will still be capable of meeting your needs in the coming years will help maximise the investment. Finally, review the requirements with the team and the operators that will be using it, to make sure everything is captured.

Once you have captured the requirements, and suppliers have submitted their proposals. Use the requirements document as a checklist to help evaluate the options. Going through each requirement one by one will objectively select the best option, and allow you to confirm the business case is acceptable.

There is an example of a requirements document included in the online resources section.

What Are the Benefits and Limitations?

- ✓ Helps understand what you need a process to do, and describe this to potential suppliers.
- ✓ Including numbers in the requirements allows easy comparison of options and confirmation of the business case and payback periods.
- ✓ Provides a checklist for acceptance testing.
- – It sometimes feels obvious which machine is required and so creating a requirements document may seem unnecessary, but even just

noting down the key volumes and other functions will be beneficial to check that the machine is a good fit.

Useful Search Terms

- Systems engineering requirements capture.
- User requirements specification (URS) for equipment.
- Techniques for requirement capture.

REQUIREMENTS CAPTURE – SOFTWARE

What Is It?

It is a method of understanding and then defining what a piece of software needs to do. This is useful to find appropriate software providers, explain what you need, and then evaluate the proposals before selecting a solution which is the best fit for your company. The approach is worthwhile when looking for off-the-shelf solutions or a bespoke system, but the level of detail of the resultant requirements document will be different. Some of the key information to gather for the requirements document is:

- Identify the issues you have with the current way of working.
- Which other systems the software will need to interact with, including details of specific file types or application programming interfaces (APIs) which allow easy data sharing between software packages.
- The areas of the business that will be included, and what is out of scope. For example, a new enterprise resource planning (ERP) system might be needed for sales, production planning, design, stock management, but not dispatch and logistics as they could already be running effective software.
- The deliverables of the project, what you want it to achieve, and what you expect it to have to cope with in the future as the business grows.
- Any hardware requirements, such as existing servers, machine controllers, or barcode scanners that the system will need to interact with, or what hardware will need to be provided by the supplier.
- The cybersecurity requirements, including how will your data be kept secure and how will your business be protected.

How Do I Do It?

Three tools that can help you start to understand your requirements are process maps ('Process Map' section), the company organisation chart, and a software architecture diagram ('Software Architecture Diagram' section). Refer to these and highlight which elements of the company the software will need to cover; they will show the limits of the system and allow you to easily discuss these with your staff. Starting the discussion with your staff early on will mean they can raise any suggestions which can be included in the specification, or highlight any concerns they have which can be addressed.

Use user stories ('User Stories' section) to gather the specific requirements from each member of staff in each area. It's unlikely that one person will know the details of every aspect of every job and what they find frustrating or difficult, which the software may be able to help with, so asking their opinions will provide valuable insights.

Summarise the findings from the user stories into a list of requirements and start to research potential solutions. If looking for off-the-shelf solutions ask for demonstrations or trial periods so you can be sure it's a good fit, and be sure to include the people who will be using the software in this. It's also worth asking about how easy it will be to customise any areas of the software which don't fit how you work. If there isn't an off-the-shelf solution available, discuss your requirements with software developers. They should help expand on the requirements document and guide you through the process of defining the system as part of the quoting process.

There is an example of a requirements document included in the online resources section.

What Are the Benefits and Limitations?

- ✓ Including staff in the process helps to identify the issues they face and increases the likelihood that the software will address these issues, and also increases the uptake once it's installed.
- ✓ Clear definition of what you need the software to do, so that the staff and suppliers know what will be included and what won't.
- – Capturing all the requirements can be a time-consuming process, especially for complex systems, so be sure to account for this when planning the approach as it's worth doing properly to avoid issues during the development and installation phases.

Useful Search Terms

- Requirements capture for <<*software type*>>.
- Requirements document for software systems.

ACCEPTANCE TESTING FOR EQUIPMENT

What Is It?

It is checking that a new machine operates as it should and meets the required specification before completing the installation. It's not unusual to complete two acceptance tests. One in the supplier's factory to identify any issues, because it will be easier to resolve them where the machine gets built. This is called the factory acceptance test (FAT). The second test is once the machine has been delivered to your factory, and is intended to check that the machine still operates correctly after being transported and installed, and that any issues identified at the FAT have been resolved. This is called the site acceptance test (SAT).

The common aspects of an acceptance test are:

- Check all safety systems operate correctly.
- Run the machine with sample components and confirm that the output is correct, and it works as defined in the requirements document, quote, or supplier proposal.
- Check all equipment and tools are included, and operate as they should.
- Check any systems that the operator uses to interact with the machine work correctly and are comfortable to use.
- Check how consumables are changed and how the maintenance or service engineer will access the areas needed.
- If there are any connections to other systems, either software or hardware, confirm that these operate correctly. This is unlikely to be possible during a FAT, but should be completed at the SAT.

The output is an agreed list of issues which need to be resolved and when these will be complete.

How Do I Do It?

Before placing the order for the equipment, agree with the supplier if you will complete both a FAT and a SAT, or just a SAT. This will depend on the complexity of the equipment, and the ease of resolving any issues that are identified. Make sure to agree a date based on the lead time of the equipment, and also if the payment terms are dependent on successfully completing the tests.

Ahead of the test inform the supplier what you intend to test and provide them with any material, tools, or fixtures that will be needed during the tests. At this point inform them who will be attending, it's usual for operators to attend and potentially maintenance engineers as well.

Use the requirements document or supplier proposal for the equipment as a checklist, and run through each line item checking that it is present or that it operates as it should.

Keep a note of any issues, and once the test is complete, agree the list of actions, who is responsible for the completion of them, and when they will be done. This is often referred to as the snag list.

There is a suggested list of tasks included in the online resource section.

What Are the Benefits and Limitations?

✓ Confirms the machine meets the requirements.

✓ Completing a FAT makes it much easier to resolve any issues.

✓ Provides confidence in the machine and introduces your staff to the machine ahead of it being installed.

– It might feel like performing acceptance tests adds unnecessary time to a project, but even off-the-shelf machines can be faulty, so running the tests identifies these as early as possible.

Useful Search Terms

• Acceptance test examples for <<*machine type*>>.

SOFTWARE ARCHITECTURE DIAGRAM

What Is It?

It is a chart showing all the different pieces of software used within the business, which areas use them, and how they link together. This is helpful when planning to implement a new software package so that it's clear which other systems it will have to interact with. It's also useful when identifying any gaps or issues in the current setup, and to provide an initial indication as to the sort of software needed to resolve these.

For example, in a typical manufacturing company it could show the sales team use emails and customer relationship management (CRM) software to keep track of orders and automatically send details to the finance package that is used by the accounting team. Elsewhere on the diagram it would show the stock management system is standalone and doesn't connect with any other systems. Production planning and order management are done on a shared spreadsheet, and this is where the team wants to make improvements. By drawing the diagram it quickly shows that any planning software they look at needs to integrate with the CRM and the stock management system.

In complex situations a number of software architecture diagrams can be created to show:

- Current state – all the areas of the business and which software packages are currently in use, highlighting the areas which are causing issues. See Figure 4.5 for an example.

- Future state – the ideal setup, showing where software will be used and where it will share data. In the planning stages it's likely that the names of the actual software aren't known, the idea is to show the intent, discuss the proposals with staff, before communicating the requirements to software providers. See Figure 4.6 for an example.

- Interim state – often it's not possible or feasible to go directly to the future state, instead there will be some initial steps. For example, if the plan is to bring in software for a number of different departments, and there isn't the resource or funding available to do it all at once, or if an over-arching ERP system is planned, which will replace many different software packages, then it makes sense to do this step by step. This could take a number of months and the business will still need to operate effectively during this time, so the interim diagrams help to plan how this will work.

How Do I Do It?

List each department or area of the business, and the software used there. This can be done on paper or on diagramming software. Discuss with the staff in the area to make sure everything is captured, and to find out what is actually used.

Add the connecting lines to show where information is shared between software packages or departments.

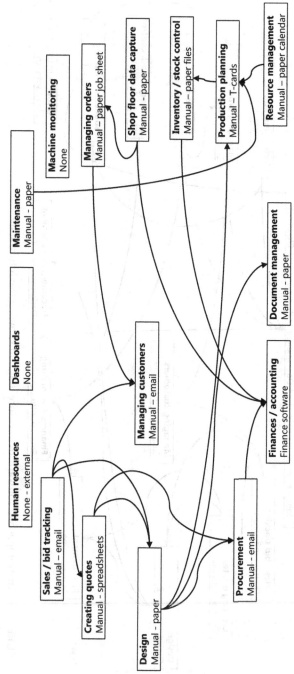

FIGURE 4.5   An example of a software architecture diagram showing the current state.

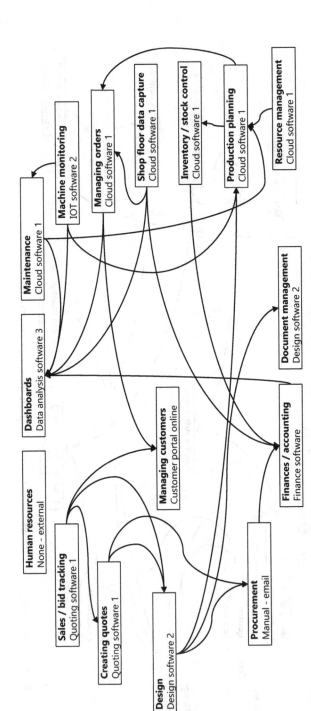

FIGURE 4.6   An example of a software architecture diagram showing the future state.

Either highlight the areas which will be the focus of the new software systems, or create a copy of the current state and update it to show the ideal state.

Use the completed diagrams to discuss with staff any other requirements, research appropriate solutions which will meet your needs, and explain to potential suppliers exactly what you need the software to do.

What Are the Benefits and Limitations?

✓ Provide clarity for staff and the management team by easily showing all the software systems, where they're used, and what they interact with.

✓ More accurate requirements capture for new systems, helping to identify issues, and enabling the supplier to create a proposal which matches your needs.

– Most companies will use a large number of software systems, and the diagram could look complex. For larger companies the diagram could be done by department, but make sure that any links to software in other departments are clearly shown, and be aware that there will be some solutions which can cover a few departments.

Useful Search Terms

- Free online diagramming tools.
- Software architecture diagram examples.
- System architecture diagram examples.
- Data flow diagram examples.

USER STORIES

What Is It?

It is a method of understanding what a user does during a particular task and then what they want a software system to do to help them. User stories are normally used in software development, in order to explain what the software needs to do for the end user without prescribing how it will be done. For a leader in a manufacturing company it can be difficult to know the details of every task in every department, and the benefit of user stories is that it allows the end user to quickly explain what they do, what works well, and what doesn't. This information can then help decide what the features of any new software need to be. The process works for either off-the-shelf or bespoke systems. See Figure 4.7 for an example.

Name:	Area:
Describe the process / task / action:	Acceptance criteria / what's the desired outcome?
How well does the current system work? 1 to 5 (1 is a big problem, 5 works well)	
How much does this affect your output? 1 to 5 (1 is a big problem, 5 works well)	Notes

FIGURE 4.7   An example of a user story form.

The elements of a user story form are:

- A description of the action or task. For example, "when I receive a new order, I copy out the details three times, once for the design department, once for accounts, and once for the customer".
- A rating of how well the current process works. In the example, this might score 3 out of 5, because it is generally reliable, but copies sometimes get lost.
- A rating of how much this impacts their output. In the example, this might score 1 out of 5, because it takes a lot of time, which could be spent on other tasks.
- A description of their desired outcome. For example, "I want to be able to accept an order by pressing one button, and the details get automatically sent to design, accounts, and the customer".

How Do I Do It?

The engagement of staff is important in ensuring accurate information. Start by explaining to the staff in the area why you want to gather the information, whether this is because you want to know which area would benefit the most from a software upgrade or because you're planning to move to a new system.

The template is straightforward, and can either be filled in by the people doing the task or by someone observing them doing it and asking for their thoughts. However, if there are a large number of tasks or operations then it can be time consuming to fill one in for every task, so decide which to focus on and group similar tasks where appropriate. If you are working with a bespoke system provider, it's likely that they will gather the user stories for you.

Once all the data has been gathered, it can be combined and analysed to build up a picture of the requirements. Where there are conflicting accounts from different people performing the same tasks, discuss the approaches with them and agree the most appropriate solution.

There is a template document included in the online resources section.

What Are the Benefits and Limitations?

✓ Understand what the software needs to do, helping to design or specify a system which will solve the problem effectively.

✓ A simple approach which can be used by anyone to find out what works and what doesn't in a process.

– For larger organisations it can be a time-consuming task due to the number of activities, but the software provider may help with it, if not, prioritise the most critical tasks or the ones which frustrate the users the most.

Useful Search Terms

• User story templates.

RESEARCH CENTRES AND THE HIGH VALUE MANUFACTURING CATAPULT

What Is It?

These are institutions which provide in-depth support from universities to businesses wanting to work with technology. University departments often provide opportunities for companies to work with them on researching and developing new materials, products, manufacturing techniques, or whatever they specialise in. This can take a number of different forms including projects for undergraduates to work on as part of their qualification, postgraduate or researcher-led studies, and industrial collaboration where a number of companies and institutions work together on a project. These can be both on a fully funded, partially funded, or on a commercial basis.

In some cases, universities set up dedicated research centres which focus on a specific technology, which provide dedicated support to businesses and often leverage local or national funding schemes to make it more accessible for small- and medium-sized enterprises (SMEs).

In the UK a national network of research centres has been established called the High Value Manufacturing Catapult,[5] with the aim of speeding up the adoption of technology by industry. These centres are run as a collaboration between universities and businesses which specialise in the relevant technologies. They allow companies to work with researchers and develop novel solutions to problems, and then test them in the centre before implementing them in their own production process. The benefits of this approach are that your business has access to the knowledge of the researchers, the equipment to develop the solution, and crucially somewhere to test the technologies without impacting production in your own facility. For companies not based in the UK, many other countries offer a similar approach.

How Do I Do It?

As an SME manufacturer it's likely that people, time, and money are precious resources, so the most important step is to decide what the problem is that you need to solve. By clearly defining what you need to achieve, when it needs to be done by, and how much time and money you have available, you make it more likely that you'll find an institution that can meet your needs. Make sure this aligns with your long-term strategy and business objectives, as these projects can often take months or even years to complete.

Once you have defined this scope, research the support which is available to you in your area, check the relevant departments at local universities, look for appropriate research centres, or a Catapult centre, or similar depending on what's available in your country.

Discuss and agree the scope and your requirements with the institution, which should include:

- Clear timescales – how long will each stage take and when will you get each deliverable.
- Deliverables – what will be provided on completion, and by whom. Will the focus be a detailed report, a simulation, or a physical trial on representative equipment, for example.

- Costs and time commitment – is there any funding available, how much will it cost you, and how much time will you be expected to commit to the project.
- Intellectual property (IP) – who will own any IP such as designs or patents at the end of the project.
- Materials and equipment – do you need to provide any raw materials, components, or tools for the project.

What Are the Benefits and Limitations?

✓ Access to equipment and knowledge that isn't available within your company.

✓ Make the most of grant funding or free support available for SMEs.

✓ Support isn't limited to manufacturing or technology, universities can provide support for other areas of the business such as marketing, e-commerce, social media, or net zero.

– If the scope, cost, and timescales aren't clearly agreed at the start then the project may not meet the business's needs, make sure to review these thoroughly before starting work.

Useful Search Terms

- University SME schemes for <<*technology area or support area*>> in <<*location*>>.
- Manufacturing research centres in <<*location*>> or <<*industry*>>.

WHERE TO FIND FUNDING

What Is It?

It is financial support which allows companies to invest in new technologies. Obtaining additional funds to invest in the company isn't restricted to retained profits or shareholders' funds. There are a number of different options; however, they vary significantly by location – this includes within a local region as well as nationally and internationally. Some examples of funding to look into are:

- Bank loans or overdrafts – traditional methods of borrowing money.
- Investors – cash investment from individuals or companies willing to provide funds for a share in the business.

- National schemes – government-created funding schemes, bids, or calls in order to increase the uptake of technology, to address challenges which are affecting the company, or to drive investment in a particular sector. These vary significantly in the amount of money available and the scope, often there will be criteria that have to be met in order to be eligible. The UK government has a funding finder tool to search for grants and support. These are usually delivered by different providers, and more details can be found on their individual websites, social media, or newsletters.

- Local schemes – regional governments or local authorities provide support for companies in order to address particular issues in their area.

- International schemes – organisations like the European Union also provide grants and other support for companies in their areas to develop and implement new technologies.

How Do I Do It?

Due to the number of different sources of support and funding, there isn't a single place to keep track of what's available for your company. They will always come with eligibility criteria and will have different application processes, such as online forms, in person visits and assessments, or competitive bids for a central pot of money. The priority for your business is to identify the greatest need or the most pressing issue which needs to be addressed, and research support that's available to help you do that. Here are some ways to find out if there's any funding available:

- In the UK there are local enterprise partnerships[6] (LEPs) operating through growth hubs, which are responsible for economic development in a particular region, and are a good source of information about what help is available for your company. For similar local advice, chambers of commerce offer a useful network of support.

- Trade organisations are usually national or international bodies set up to represent a particular industry; they are a good source of information specific to the industries you operate in and if there are funding or support schemes available.

- National governments will advertise the funding calls that they are running, usually through their central website.

- Universities and research centres are more likely to offer funded projects covering researcher time and materials, but in some cases they will be part of a larger scheme offering funding for equipment and software as well. Many university courses also offer student placements which is a good way of introducing new skills into the business as an initial trial.
- Accountants deal with many different clients and are often aware of the funding opportunities available.

What Are the Benefits and Limitations?

✓ Reduced risk, increased scope, or an improved payback period for new projects.

✓ Networking through these institutions may lead to new opportunities.

– There isn't a single source of information about the funding opportunities available, so it's best to keep in touch with a number of the institutions.

– The funding isn't guaranteed so ideally the project's business case should stand up on its own, without the funding, but in some cases this isn't possible which is why grants are made available.

Useful Search Terms

- Local/national funding for SMEs in <<location>>.
- <<Industry>> trade organisation.

WHERE TO GO FOR TECHNICAL SUPPORT

What Is It?

It is the process of getting help with the technical elements of a project from external organisations. Companies rarely have all the skills they need within their staff, especially when new technology or systems are being planned, implemented, and used. This is even more noticeable with smaller companies, for example, it is unrealistic for a bakery employing 20 people to have specialists that know everything about the packing machines, the order management system, finance software, and the e-commerce site. It's likely that the bakery has a person who can resolve some issues with the packing machines, and someone else who's more familiar with order management and can solve problems with that. But when they don't have the answers, they can call a service engineer to look at the machines, or customer support from the software provider for help. This will be even more noticeable when the bakery is looking to invest in new technology, as it's unlikely to have access to a specialist in augmented reality or robotics. Technical support is available in these instances, to provide advice on guidance on how to proceed.

How Do I Do It?

The first step is to clarify what support you need and what you want to get out of it, for example, do you need help getting a proposal for a fully automatic processing line, or do you want to try virtual reality to see how it could be applied to your business – the level of support will be different. Here are some options:

- Trade organisations and trade shows provide a good introduction to how technologies can be applied in specific industries, as well as allowing you to speak to a number of suppliers to help you understand what's possible and what isn't.
- Suppliers of the equipment or systems will provide advice, often visiting to understand your requirements better. They'll be able to give you indications of costs and benefits to help build up your business case for new technologies.
- Research institutions and universities often provide funded or subsidised support and advice to SME manufacturers. For more detailed work or for cutting edge technology development they can support on a commercial basis. See 'Universities and Research Centres' section.
- Consultants offer specialist advice and services – the benefit is that they have experience and knowledge in a particular field, the downside is that it can be expensive, but this should be included in the business case of adopting the technology as a way of reducing the risks of the project.

What Are the Benefits and Limitations?

- ✓ Initial advice and support can be free to help with an introduction to a topic.
- ✓ Attending trade shows and working with research centres can help with networking and open up other opportunities for the business.

✓ Reduces the risk of adopting technology by exploring different options and getting other opinions.

– A company can become reliant on one or two suppliers or consultants, so make sure to look at skills and knowledge within the business and develop skill sets internally where necessary using a skills matrix ('Skills Matrix' section) or succession planning ('Succession Planning' section).

Useful Search Terms

- <<*Industry*>> trade organisation.
- <<*Technology type*>> consultant in <<*industry*>> or <<*location*>>.
- Manufacturing research centres in <<*industry*>> or <<*location*>>.

NOTES

1 *5S what is the 5S methodology?* Lean Production. (August 2023). www.leanproduction.com/5s/

2 Womack, JP and Jones, DT. *Lean thinking, banish waste and create wealth in your corporation.* Simon & Schuster, 1997.

3 *APM resources.* Association for Project Management. (August 2023). www.apm.org.uk/resources/

4 *What is agile project management?* Association for Project Management. (August 2023). www.apm.org.uk/resources/find-a-resource/agile-project-management/

5 *Transforming manufacturing together.* High Value Manufacturing Catapult. (August 2023). https://hvm.catapult.org.uk/

6 *The LEP network.* LEP Network. (July 2023). www.lepnetwork.net/

BIBLIOGRAPHY

Association for Project Management. *APM body of knowledge 7th edition.* 2019.

Association for Project Management. *APM resources.* August 2023. Available at http://www.apm.org.uk/resources/

Association for Project Management. *What is agile project management?* August 2023. http://www.apm.org.uk/resources/find-a-resource/agile-project-management/

High Value Manufacturing Catapult. *Transforming manufacturing together.* August 2023. https://hvm.catapult.org.uk/

Lean Production. *5S what is the 5S methodology?* August 2023. Available at http://www.leanproduction.com/5s/

Lean Six Sigma Definition. *5S.* August 2023. Available at http://www.leansixsigmadefinition.com/glossary/5s/

LEP Network. *The LEP network.* July 2023. www.lepnetwork.net/5S.

SCANBA. *Experimental design online.* August 2023. Available at https://experimental design.online/

Womack, JP and Jones, DT. *Lean thinking, banish waste and create wealth in your corporation.* Simon & Schuster, 1997.

CHAPTER 5

Tools vs Technology Matrix, and Common Issues

TOOLS VS TECHNOLOGY MATRIX

What Is It?

It is a look up table to match technologies with the appropriate tools which will be useful in scoping the right solution and implementing it correctly. See Figure 5.1.

How Do I Do It?

Find the technology that you're interested in implementing along the top of the table and follow the column down to see which tools and techniques will help you with the project. A copy is included in the online resources section.

Where a tool is marked with • it means this is strongly recommended to make the project a success.

Where a tool is marked with ○ it means this could be useful, depending on the project.

Where a tool is marked with ◊ it means this is useful on larger or more complex projects.

The tools from Chapter 1 are recommended for any business, regardless of whether adopting technology is a priority or not. However, there

DOI: 10.1201/9781032642215-6

Column headers (top, rotated):
- Virtual reality
- Smart glasses
- Factory simulation, process simulation and human factors simulation
- Digital twin, augmented reality, mixed reality, extended reality
- Warehouse management
- Supervisory control and data acquisition (SCADA)
- Net zero / carbon / sustainability
- Radio frequency identification (RFID)
- Key process variable control
- Energy monitoring and modelling (IoT)
- Building information modelling
- Industrial internet of things (IIoT)
- Cloud computing
- 4G and 5G network or private networks
- AR learning
- Blockchain
- Stock / inventory management
- Shop floor data capture
- Sales / demand forecasting
- Resource management
- Quality management
- Process tracking
- Order tracking
- Manufacturing resource planning
- Systems software
- Finance software
- Data database / accounting
- Customer portals / accounting
- Customer relationship management
- CRM
- Customer resource planning
- Enterprise resource planning
- Geolocation
- Warehouse automation
- Vision systems and machine automation
- Robotics
- Autonomation
- Big data
- Artificial intelligence and machine learning
- Additive manufacturing or 3D printing

Row labels (left):
- Company strategy / business plan
- Technology strategy
- Key performance indicators and metrics
- Building a business case
- Roles and responsibilities
- Succession planning
- Change management
- Skills matrix
- 5S
- Design of experiments and statistical analysis
- Lean manufacturing
- Overall equipment effectiveness (OEE)
- Process input / output diagram
- Process map
- Standard operating procedure
- Value stream map
- Project management or agile project management
- Network diagram
- Gantt chart
- Life cycle analysis
- Risk management
- Requirements capture – hardware
- Requirements capture – software
- Acceptance testing
- Software architecture diagram
- User stories
- Research centres and the High Value Manufacturing Catapult

Key:
●	Strongly recommended to support the project
○	May be useful / likely to support the project
⊘	Useful for complex or high value projects

FIGURE 5.1 The tools and technology matrix.

could be situations where it is appropriate to continue with a low-risk project without formally completing these, although they should still be considered or discussed as a leadership team beforehand to check the project is in line with the business's plans.

COMMON ISSUES AND SUGGESTED STEPS

Manufacturing leaders often face similar issues and challenges when running their businesses. While these will vary depending on several factors such as the age of the company, industry, staff, culture and location, standard tools and technologies can be applied to resolve them.

Company Information Is on Different Systems That Don't Talk to Each Other

Start by noting down which software is used by each area of the business, and where data can currently be shared. Use a software architecture diagram ('Software Architecture Diagram' section) to show how it currently works and to show how it would ideally work.

Gather the requirements for any new software, changes to existing software, or instructions for a software developer see 'Requirements Capture – Software' section and complete user stories ('User Stories' section).

Refer to the software sections in the technologies section for more detail about specific modules, see sections 'Enterprise Resource Planning (ERP) through to 'Stock or Inventory Management'.

Current Software Systems Are Out of Date or Unsupported

It may be possible to upgrade your current software to a newer version from the same supplier, or it may be that there is now a better-suited software system available. Either way, gather the requirements for what you need the software to do for you ('Requirements Capture – Software' section) and complete user stories ('User Stories' section).

Refer to the software sections in the technologies section for more detail about specific modules, see sections 'Enterprise Resource Planning (ERP) through to 'Stock or Inventory Management'.

Discuss these requirements with your current provider, and research any alternative suppliers, before evaluating which is the best fit for your business. Consider the data on your current system and produce a strategy for how the new system will be implemented and what data will be transferred.

Energy Costs Are Too High

Low cost sensors can quickly show the power use, and cost, of running individual machines see 'Energy Monitoring' section and 'Industrial Internet of Things' section. Collecting the data is the first step, and will allow you to identify which are the most efficient machines and when they are most costly to run.

Developing a net zero plan will also help reduce energy costs, while also making the business more resilient to energy cost increases or supply issues, see 'Net Zero' section.

Keeping Track of Material or Stock Is Time Consuming

Stock management software or a stock control module in an enterprise resource planning (ERP) system will help to monitor and control inventory, see 'Stock or Inventory Management' section and 'Enterprise Resource Planning' section.

Gather the requirements for any new software, changes to existing software, or instructions for a software developer see 'Requirements Capture – Software' section and complete user stories ('User Stories' section). Use a software architecture diagram ('Software Architecture Diagram' section) to show how the new software will share data with any existing systems.

Keeping Track of Orders Is Difficult

Customer relationship management software ('Customer Relationship Management' section), customer portals ('Customer Portals section), order tracking ('Order Tracking' section), and shop floor data capture (SDFC) ('Shop Floor Data Capture' section) can all help to organise the data from each order and make it accessible to anyone who needs to see it.

Gather the requirements for any new software, changes to existing software, or instructions for a software developer see 'Requirements Capture – Software' section and complete user stories ('User Stories' section). Use a software architecture diagram ('Software Architecture Diagram' section) to show how the new software will share data with any existing systems.

Paper Systems Cause a Lot of Errors or Are Time Consuming

Software is available which will replace all paper systems, but it may not be appropriate or feasible to implement a completely digital process straightaway. Use a process map ('Process Map' section) to set out the sequence of tasks involved in each area of the business, and then identify which areas have problems with paper systems. An enterprise resource planning (ERP) system ('Enterprise Resource Planning' section) will cover most areas of the business, whereas individual modules are available which will help with specific areas, see sections 'Customer Relationship Management' to 'Stock or Inventory Management'.

Gather the requirements for any new software, changes to existing software, or instructions for a software developer see 'Requirements Capture – Software' and complete user stories ('User Stories' section). Use a software architecture diagram ('Software Architecture Diagram' section) to show how the new software will share data with any existing systems.

It's Difficult to Manage a Large Number of Product Variants

A number of different software solutions can help with this, depending on which area of the business has this problem. Computer-aided design (CAD) and product life cycle management (PLM) will help during the design phase, and by creating modular components with design rules and design automation, variations can be managed more easily ('Computer Aided Design' section). In other areas of the business enterprise resource planning (ERP) ('Enterprise Resource Planning' section), manufacturing resource planning (MRP) ('Manufacturing Resource Planning' section), production planning ('Production Planning' section), order tracking ('Order Tracking' section), and stock management (see 'Stock or Inventory Management' section) may be helpful.

Gather the requirements for any new software, changes to existing software, or instructions for a software developer see 'Requirements Capture – Software' section and complete user stories ('User Stories' section). Use a software architecture diagram ('Software Architecture Diagram' section) to show how the new software will share data with any existing systems.

Our Systems Require a Lot of Repetitive Data Entry

This happens when software systems from different providers are in use, but the information in each one can't be shared easily. If the software systems work well and you don't want to change to a new service, speak to a software developer about linking the systems using application programming interfaces (API), a custom program, or through a workflow automation or automated integration service. Alternatively, investigate a new system which will perform all the tasks, or a set of software solutions which can be easily integrated or can easily share the data.

Create a process map ('Process Map' section) to identify where the systems need to be linked and what data needs to be shared, and a software architecture diagram ('Software Architecture Diagram' section) will show how the systems will need to interact. Gather the requirements for any new software, changes to existing software, or instructions for a software developer see 'Requirements Capture – Software' section and complete user stories ('User Stories' section).

Do I Need a Single Enterprise Resource Planning (ERP) System or Individual Services?

A single enterprise resource planning (ERP) system see 'Enterprise Resource Planning' section will include modules for each area of the business and aims to streamline their processes while making data accessible to anyone who needs it. This can be a complex process which takes time and may involve upgrades of hardware and training for every member of staff.

Alternatively, individual software services can be implemented one by one, eventually replicating everything that an ERP system does. Where one software system is incompatible with another, automation services can be used to handle the data transfer. The benefits of this approach are that the best software provider can be selected for each area of the business, and they can be installed as they're needed, making it more manageable. However, the result can be a complex mix of different software providers and licences, and data sharing between the systems needs to be a priority.

The best fit will depend on your company, experience, and software requirements. Use a process map ('Process Map' section) for each business area to understand requirements, and capture them in a requirements document ('Requirements Capture – Software' section) and user stories ('User Stories' section). A current and future-state software architecture diagram ('Software Architecture Diagram' section) will help to evaluate the complexity of each option as well as identifying what data needs to be shared.

Skilled Staff Spend a Lot of Time Performing Unskilled Tasks

Automating processes can free up time for skilled staff to focus on more value-added activities. This can be with software or machinery. Create a process map ('Process Map' section) to identify where the main issues occur. For physical processes, see 'Automation' section and use a requirements document to specify what you need it to do ('Requirements Capture – Hardware' section). For software gather the requirements for any new software, changes to existing software, or instructions for a software developer, see Requirements Capture – Software section and complete user stories ('User Stories' section).

Supply Chain Lead Times Are Too Long

There is risk in even simple supply chains, with uncertainty affecting delivery times and supplier performance, but there are ways to reduce the risk of disruption and the impact if it does happen. Review the company's business strategy ('Company Strategy' section) and identify if any key suppliers or product lines are the issue, and bring alternative suppliers online or investigate modular design to reduce the risk and improve flexibility. Technology such as artificial intelligence and machine learning ('Artificial Intelligence' section) can be used to identify trends in sales profiles and improve forecasting; this could be part of a customer relationship management software solution ('Customer Relationship Management' section) or an enterprise resource planning (ERP) solution ('Enterprise Resource Planning' section). Stock management systems ('Stock or Inventory Management' section), manufacturing resource planning (MRP) software ('Manufacturing Resource Planning' section), and logistics planning software ('Logistics Planning' section) can also help manage components and materials in the supply chain.

We Don't Know How Much Our Products Cost to Make or Which Are Profitable

Use manufacturing resource planning MRP software ('Manufacturing Resource Planning' section) to track each item in a bill of materials (BoM), how much they cost, improve production planning, and monitor production times. Individual modules such as production planning ('Production Planning' section), order tracking ('Order Tracking' section), and shop floor data capture ('Shop Floor Data Capture' section) can also help, without implementing a full MRP solution.

Create a process map ('Process Map' section) to explain how your business operates, and a software architecture diagram ('Software Architecture Diagram' section) to show how the systems will need to interact. Gather the requirements for any new software, changes to existing software, or instructions for a software developer ('Requirements Capture – Software' section) and complete user stories ('User Stories' section).

Staff Don't Have Quick Access to Information They Need

The type of information the staff need to access will determine the most appropriate type of software solution, see the software sections in the technologies chapter for more detail about specific modules, see sections 'Enterprise Resource Planning' through to 'Stock or Inventory Management'. For staff based on different sites or working from home, a cloud solution will allow them to work from anywhere with an internet connection, see 'Cloud Computing' section.

Gather the requirements for any new software, changes to existing software, or instructions for a software developer (see 'Requirements Capture – Software' section) and complete user stories ('User Stories' section). Use a software architecture diagram ('Software Architecture Diagram' section) to show how the new software will share data with any existing systems.

I Don't Have Enough Time to Spend on Important Tasks

Use a skills matrix ('Skills Matrix' section) to identify people who can support you with specific tasks, and increase the amount you can delegate to them, so you can focus on your priorities, although it's important to consider their workload at the same time. There are also time management techniques in the 'Time Management' section.

I Don't Know Which Project to Prioritise

Start with the company strategy and business plan ('Company Strategy' section) and create a technology strategy or roadmap ('Technology Strategy' section) to clearly show what the business needs to do in the coming months or years. Once these are complete, score each project against how well they will help the company achieve its goals. Include other measures to make this selection process more thorough, such as likely costs, timescales, probability of success, and the amount of time staff will have to spend on it.

Critical Company Knowledge Sits with One Person or Key People Are Approaching Retirement

Look at succession planning ('Succession Planning' section) and create a skills matrix ('Skills Matrix' section) to show which person is capable of which task and include important company knowledge as a category for each area. Once it's complete, review the matrix to identify who is in the best position to transfer the knowledge and skills to. This helps when employees are approaching retirement and will make the business more resilient by ensuring the information is kept within the business. Creating process maps ('Process Map' section) can also be useful to understand the sequence of tasks, look at who is capable of performing them, then create standard operating procedures ('Standard Operating Procedures' section) to embed this knowledge in the process.

It Is Difficult to Recruit and Retain Staff or We Have a High Staff Turnover

Speak to current staff to get an understanding of what people like and don't like about the work, see 'Employee Retention' section. A diversity and inclusion policy ('Equality, Diversity and Inclusion' section) and an employee engagement survey can make the workplace feel more inviting and accommodating, make sure to get feedback from staff on the outcomes and any planned changes. Use a skills matrix ('Skills Matrix' section), roles and responsibilities ('Roles and Responsibilities' section), and succession planning ('Succession Planning' section) to provide staff with options for career progression and personal development. Sharing the plans for the business ('Company Strategy' section) and change management ('Change Management' section) will also help staff to understand what the business is going to do in the future and reduce uncertainty.

It's Difficult to Schedule Production or Production Plans Are Never Met

Create a process map ('Process Map' section) of the manufacturing operations, and a skills matrix ('Skills Matrix' section) to show who can do what task and to help manage shift cover. Software modules for production planning ('Production Planning' section), manufacturing resource planning ('Manufacturing Resource Planning' section), and stock or inventory management ('Stock or Inventory Management' section) can also help.

It's important to identify the reasons why scheduling is difficult, and address the issues. Tools such as value stream maps ('Value Stream Map' section), lean manufacturing ('Lean Manufacturing' section), and overall equipment effectiveness ('Overall Equipment Effectiveness' section) can help with this.

We Have High Scrap or Rework Levels

First set a standard for what is acceptable at each operation, to ensure that products aren't being scrapped or marked for rework unnecessarily, when the customer or downstream process would accept them. If a process is too unpredictable, use a process input/output diagram ('Process Input/ Output Diagram' section) to identify what needs to be controlled in order to improve the quality of the products. For more precise operations use design of experiments ('Design of Experiments' section) to accurately show what the important aspects of a process are and then what the tolerance limits are. Lean manufacturing techniques ('Lean Manufacturing' section), 5S ('5S' section), and standard operating procedures ('Standard Operating Procedures' section) can also be used to improve quality.

We Don't Know How Efficient Production Is

Shop floor data capture (SDFC) systems ('Shop Floor Data Capture' section) can be used to gather information from operators or machines, similarly applying sensors to machines and equipment can provide valuable information see 'Industrial Internet of Things' section. Once the data is captured it needs to be analysed, which will be included in the package offered by most suppliers of sensors or SFDC systems, but it could also be useful to bring data together from different sources and display it on screens or dashboards in each area of the business, see 'Data Dashboards' section.

Production Is Repetitive or Manual

Investigate automation ('Automation' section) for particular tasks in your production process. Use a process map ('Process Map' section) to explain the steps in production and to help identify which tasks are most suitable for automation. Research products that are available, there may be off the shelf machines which can perform individual elements and are easier to implement than automating everything. Use a skills matrix ('Skills Matrix' section), process input/output diagram ('Process Input/Output Diagram' section), and a requirements document ('Requirements Capture – Hardware' section) to understand exactly what you need the machine to do. For larger projects a technology strategy ('Technology Strategy' section), change management ('Change Management' section), and a business case ('Building a Business Case' section) will help your staff to understand what is going to happen and what their role will be in the future, which will improve the likelihood of success.

Creating Quotes for Customised Products Is Time Consuming

Specific software is available to support the quoting process, in particular with complex products or large projects which involve tendering processes. Use a process map ('Process Map' section) to understand how your company approaches this, and standardise it as much as possible. A requirements document ('Requirements Capture – Software' section) will help you to understand exactly what you need the software to do, and to evaluate potential solutions. Alternatively, systems such as enterprise resource planning ('Enterprise Resource Planning' section) or order tracking ('Order Tracking' section) may include features which will improve the quoting process. Linking any of these with the design process using computer-aided design ('Computer Aided Design' section) could help to make transferring information between departments easier, and using artificial intelligence ('Artificial Intelligence' section) can help with creation of the quotes or marketing material.

Demonstrating Products to Potential Customers Is Expensive

Augmented reality ('Augmented Reality' section) or virtual reality systems ('Virtual Reality' section) can use data from computer-aided design ('Computer Aided Design' section) software to create realistic demonstrations using either a dedicated headset or a device like a mobile phone or tablet. Once set up it could quickly switch between different products or model variants to show the benefits, and give customers an idea of what your product would look like in their facility or home. Use a requirements document ('Requirements Capture – Software' section) to show suppliers what you need the system to do, and to evaluate options.

Keeping in Touch with Customers Is Difficult

Customer relationship management software ('Customer Relationship Management' section) is designed to log every communication you have with your customers, and often links with email systems or other software solutions to automatically track this. Having these data in one place allows you to analyse which customers haven't ordered for a certain amount of time, if there are any trends in their orders, or if there are other services you can offer them to increase the number of orders. Artificial intelligence ('Artificial Intelligence' section) can also be used to help create marketing emails personalised for particular customers, or to create content such as newsletters aimed at certain markets or groups of customers. Use a process map ('Process Map' section) and a requirements document ('Requirements Capture – Software' section) to show suppliers what you need the system to do, and to evaluate options.

Glossary

4G/5G: fourth and fifth generation of mobile network technology, each generation offers increased communication speeds, bandwidth, and reliability.

Application programming interface (API): a method of quickly and securely sharing data between software packages.

Circular economy: designing and manufacturing a product with the intent of extending its useful life as long as possible, by enabling its reuse, repair, recycling, and refurbishment.[1]

Computer numerical control (CNC): using a computer program to automatically control the movement and operation of a machine.

Cryptocurrency: a digital currency which uses blockchain technology to enable to the sale and transfer of funds.

Ecommerce: buying or selling products online through your own website, or through a third-party system.

General data protection regulation (GDPR): laws relating to how personal data is stored and processed by companies, individuals, and other organisations.[2]

Integrator: a company which provides technology solutions by combining products from third parties. A software integrator specialises in implementing software from different providers. A hardware integrator specialises in equipment from different producers, for instance, combining a robot, robot controller, gripper, safety system, and programming software to create a fully operational robot cell.

LoRaWAN: a wireless communication technology used in the industrial internet of things (IIoT), similar to WiFi but with lower power requirements and a longer range.

Meta data: additional information included in a file, for example, the location of where a photograph was taken can be embedded in an image file.

Net present value: a method of comparing the costs and monetary benefits of different projects over their full lifetime.

Original equipment manufacturer (OEM): the company which made the machine or product in the first instance, as opposed to a third-party supplier of spare parts, for example.

Programmable logic controller (PLC): the computer which controls the operation of a machine, and often allows the collection of data about its operation and performance.

Quick response (QR) code: a 2D barcode which is capable of holding more information than a traditional barcode made of stripes.

Return on investment: a measure of how well a project will pay back the initial investment.

Risks: events which may or may not happen, but if they do, they will affect the outcome of the project in some way.

Small- and medium-sized enterprise (SME): companies with less than 250 employees, and either a turnover of less than €50m or a balance sheet total of less than €43m.[3]

Stakeholder: anybody with an interest or involvement in a project or company, or somebody who may be affected by it. They could be internal, such as employees, managers, or someone from a different department, or they could be external, such as suppliers, the local community, customers, or government organisations.

Supply chain: all the suppliers and customers involved in getting your products to the end user.[4]

Value chain: where value is added to your products as it progress through the supply chain.[5]

NOTES

1 *What is the circular economy?* European Parliament. (September 2023). www.europarl.europa.eu/news/en/headlines/economy/20151201STO05603/circular-economy-definition-importance-and-benefits

2 EU General Data Protection Regulation (GDPR): Regulation (EU) 2016/679. http://data.europa.eu/eli/reg/2016/679/2016-05-04

3 *SME definition.* European Commission. (September 2023). https://single-market-economy.ec.europa.eu/smes/sme-definition_en

4 *What is a value chain? Definitions and characteristics.* University of Cambridge. (September 2023). www.cisl.cam.ac.uk/education/graduate-study/pgcerts/value-chain-defs

5 *What is a value chain? Definitions and characteristics.* University of Cambridge. (September 2023). www.cisl.cam.ac.uk/education/graduate-study/pgcerts/value-chain-defs

BIBLIOGRAPHY

European Commission. *SME definition.* September 2023. Available at https://single-marketeconomy.ec.europa.eu/smes/sme-definition_en

EU General Data Protection Regulation (GDPR): Regulation (EU) 2016/679. Available at http://data.europa.eu/eli/reg/2016/679/2016-05-04

European Parliament. *What is the circular economy?* September 2023. Available at www.europarl.europa.eu/news/en/headlines/economy/20151201STO05603/circulareconomy-definition-importance-and-benefits

University of Cambridge. *What is a value chain? Definitions and characteristics.* September 2023. Available at www.cisl.cam.ac.uk/education/graduate-study/pgcerts/value-chain-defs

Index

Note: Figures are indicated by *Italics*.

Printed in the United States
by Baker & Taylor Publisher Services

Printed in the United States
by Baker & Taylor Publisher Services